Anonymous

Strictures on the Letter of the Right Hon. Mr. Burke

On the Revolution in France

Anonymous

Strictures on the Letter of the Right Hon. Mr. Burke
On the Revolution in France

ISBN/EAN: 9783337016579

Printed in Europe, USA, Canada, Australia, Japan

Cover: Foto ©ninafisch / pixelio.de

More available books at **www.hansebooks.com**

STRICTURES

ON THE

LETTER

OF THE

Right Hon. Mr. BURKE,

ON THE

REVOLUTION IN FRANCE.

Haec cùm loqueris, nos barones ſtupemus : tu videlicet tecum ipſe vides.
Cicer. de Fin. Bonor. et Malor. Lib. ii. *cap.* 23.

—— Liberty cannot be preſerved long by any people, who do not preſerve that watchful and jealous *ſpirit* of Liberty, on the neceſſity of which I have inſiſted. If you are once convinced of this truth, you will know what opinion to entertain of thoſe, who endeavour to extinguiſh this ſpirit, and of thoſe, who do all they can to keep it alive.
Bolingbroke, Rem. on the Hiſt. of Eng. Letter ii. *p.* 20.

LONDON:

Printed for H. GARDNER, oppoſite St. Clement's Church, Strand, 1791.

ERRATA.

Page	line	
12	2	the note, for λοϐοι, read λαϐοι
14	14	for Socrates, read Iſocrates
26	5 from bottom,	for accompany, read accompanied
29	10	for heaven, read Heaven
—	15	for principal, read Principal
—	16	for his, read His
—	17	for his, read His
30	11	for des ſpeculation, read de ſpeculation
36	4 from bottom,	for ϐασιλευιν, read ϐασιλευειν
43	10 from bottom	for praeſtantia, read praeſtantior
49	3	for quofque, read quoque
59	ult.	for to be ſupported, read to be ſo ſupported
—	5	the note, for cisì, read cioè—and for dell' miniſtri, read delli miniſtri
—	6	the note, for quito, read queſto.
61	3	the note, for ſubtile, read ſubtle
63	2	the note, after *riches* put a femicolon
—	6	the note, for eicelò, read eccitò
—	2	the note, from bottom, for traver, read haver
—	ult.	the note, for dopa read dopo
64	4	the note, for altra perſonne, read altre perſone
—	4	the note, from bottom, for facundo, read facendo
—	3	the note, from bottom, for acreſculi, read accreſcerli
68	1	for κηροχϑηναι, read κηρυχϑηναι
—	6 from bottom,	for praeteribo, read praeteribo
—	4 from bottom,	for conſperit, read conſpexit
69	16	for ſencerim, read ſenſerim
71	4 from bottom,	for concluded, read excluded
75	2	the note, from bottom, for face read fare
80	4	for inſtitutions, read inſtitution
—	11	for boaſt, read beaſt
—	13	for dolls, read dolts
82	5	for accompliſhments, read accompaniments
87	4 from bottom,	for durations, read deviations
88	4	for modules, read moduſes
—	13	dele *con*
97	10	for acquora, read aequora
98	7 from bottom	for princes, read Princes!
—	ult.	for dream, breaks, read dream, he breaks
101	11	for politeſſe, read petiteſſe
—	2 from bottom	for miſteries, read myſteries
106		the note, after *Men*, inſert " by a Woman."
118	12	for of, read off
124	7	dele the firſt *and* —— line 9, for that, read the
——	4 from bottom,	for lie, read be
126	3	the note, for danoro, read danaro
——	4	for die, read dei
——	5	for danoro, read danaro
——	6	for anco, read anco
127	4	the note, for quantenque, read quantunque
——	13	for igni, read ogni
——	ult.	for rilener, read ritener
128	2	the note, for aureſculi, read accreſcerli
——	6	for lecinio, read Licinio
129	1	for ottenue, read ottenne
——	2	for d'alceni, read d'alcuni
——	10	for gle, read gli
——	13	for cornuttione, read corruttione
——	14	for Poce, read Pochi
130	5	the note, for lilerici muſanti, read li Chierici mercanti
——	10	for Coro, read loro
132	9	for object, read objects
133	12	for ſignal, read ſignat
——	8	the note, for pumeteſſe, read permetteſſe

STRICTURES.

MR. BURKE's letter, containing "Reflections on the Revolution in France, &c." had passed into the hands of the greater part of his readers, had, I believe, been answered by many, and probably was laid afide, before I could be prevailed on to give it a reading; nor would this at length have been complied with, but at the interceffion of a friend, to whom I can refufe nothing. My reafon for this coolnefs originated in having for fome time paft difcovered, as I conceived, an evident defalcation in that gentleman's political principles, principles which did him honour, and gained him reputation as a fpeaker; the exchange he has made coincided not with my fentiments, and it was with reluctance that I yielded myfelf once more to be entangled in the fophiftry of an eccentric

centric genius levelled with such facility, and as it were for amusement played off against reason, and with his leave, the rights of men. His performance is long and tedious, or it might seem to partake of those qualities only to me, who am verging towards old age, and who found there among some matter useful and entertaining, much to condemn as revolting against *his* former sentiments, as well as my own. Impressed with this idea, though labouring under many disadvantages, and apprized that many able writers had answered that publication, yet I could not refrain from casting in my mite to obstruct, if not to stem, the ravages that some of those opinions might make on the minds of mankind; in doing this, I have adhered to my own feelings and sentiments, regardless of what may have been advanced by others. But before I proceed in this undertaking, I judge it necessary to profess my sincerity; that I am actuated by no private motive, that I have no pique or sinister view to promote, and that I engage in it from pure benevolence with the hope of promoting, though in a small degree, the happiness of my fellow creatures.

I must here premise, that controversy is for the most part not only unpleasant, but unprofitable;

able; it generally decides nothing. It is principally employed on abstract ideas, and the matter affirmed or denied concerning them, very rarely admits of unequivocal demonstration or proof. All controversy would be soon dispatched and determined, or rather there would be no cause for controversy, could we proceed in the like manner and with the same certainty as when discoursing on figures and lines. No person competent to the question doubts whether $4 \times 4 = 16$, or whether each angle of an equilateral triangle be equal to either of the other two; the reason is, that the term or figure 4 contains or represents in the opinion of all men conversant with it, one immutable invariable known quantity; this being immutably fixed, the rest follows of course; or if doubted, the proof might easily be adduced, for those who did not perceive it carried its proof along with it: and the like may be said of the angles of an equilateral triangle. But if men doubted, or were of different opinions concerning the quantity represented by the figure 4, some imputing to it a less, and some a greater quantity, from this uncertainty endless controversy would arise in discoursing concerning it, nor could it be adjusted till some fixed and determined quantity were appropriated to it by universal consent.

In difcourfing therefore on abftract ideas from the want of fuch determination, controverfies are not only multiplied, but they have no end. Logicians have in vain endeavoured to remedy this defect, by fubftituting definitions. No definition can be fo conftructed as to excite in the mind of another, that precife and clear perception of any abftract idea, nor indeed of any thing elfe, which every competent perfon entertains of the quantity reprefented by the figure 4, or by any other figure. Befides, in treating of abftract ideas, mankind are rarely agreed in the component parts; fuppofe virtue for example, fome men impute to it more, fome fewer qualities, others again different qualities, fubtracting, retaining, or adding and modifying, ad infinitum, agreeably to their own conceits or opinions; fo that unlefs all men were perfectly agreed in the definition, as precifely as they are in the quantity reprefented by the figure, the definition is ufelefs, and confequently the controverfy concerning virtue, or any other abftract idea, becomes endlefs, and undecifive. This uncertainty arifing from deficiency of proof and demonftration attendant on abftraction, has, at different times, incited eccentric geniufes to ftart new and ftrange doctrines, or to revive and varnifh up the old, not with a view to fup-

port

port the cause of truth and humanity, but to acquire to themselves celebrity and fame; and in case controversy should arise, they have always an asylum in the imbecility of human reason, destitute of those powers which are requisite to convince by infallible proof and demonstration. Hence so many opposite doctrines on the same points are seen subsisting in the world, and ever will be, for human reasonings are but judgments and opinions, often erroneous, and seldom or never supported by absolute proof and certainty; controversies, therefore, when settled, are determined by the preponderating weight or number of opinions; could they be concluded on principles of indubitable demonstration and proof, no controversy could subsist for a day; all erroneous reasonings, judgments and opinions, would instantaneously flee before this light of truth, and be consigned to darkness and permanent oblivion. Thus much is premised, that it may not be expected of me to advance nothing without proof, while Mr. B. has produced no proof, that I see, for any thing he has advanced. We have, indeed, his doubts, conjectures, inuendoes, half-explained wishes, desultory arguments, and false deductions and conclusions; but we have not even that authority which might have been

obtained

obtained for many of the facts he mentions; some of which, however boldly afferted, are extremely queftionable. My age has rendered me too experienced to rely on the ipfe dixit of any man where I can difcover evident partiality, and he muft pardon me if I do not give full credit to *all* he relates.

It gave me no fmall concern to obferve a vein of acrimony pervade his whole letter, pointed directly againft the Revolution in France, its authors and abettors, wherever to be found, without any regard to their moral characters or abilities; the national affembly treated with indignant perfonalities; and moft of their operations and meafures, without referve or diftinction condemned. The tone affumed, the enthufiaftic emotions, the prefumed knowledge, from a long ftudy of men and things, with other extraneous and extravagant matter might command a fmile or excite our pity. But when he prefumptuoufly derides what is of the laft importance, the execution of which is fo vaft as to defy all the powers of the human mind to accomplifh at once, to make no allowance for human imbecility in what he conceives to be error, but to confole himfelf in the future mifcarriage of a plan concerted to reftore twenty-
five

(9)

five millions of the human species to freedom; when we behold this unfriendly disposition, we are justified in questioning the purity of his candour, the validity of his assertions, the power of his assumed abilities, and to give him no longer credit for any more of these accomplishments and qualities, than are evidently stamped as his with the unerring seals of justice and truth.

Under what appellation we are to speak of the form of government established or establishing in France is immaterial; it is however to be denominated a mixed form of government, its component parts are limited monarchy, and, as I apprehend, a timocracy. The latter is treated of by Aristotle in his Ethics, lib. viii. c. 10. τρίτη δ'η απο τιμηματων, ην τιμοκρατην λεγειν οικειον φαινεται; it differs from a democracy which admits all the citizens to a share in government, but the timocracy such only as pay a tax or have an income; the democracy respects *person*, the timocracy *person* and *property*. This mixed with a limited monarchy, is a form of government which I believe no where existed before; but it is not to be condemned or censured on this account, for the same may be alleged of the mixed form of our English Government, the like

B having

having never before exifted in any nation, nor does it exift in any kingdom but our own, yet mankind are far from faying that it comes under the denomination of thofe forms of government which are accounted bad; nor will any but rafh and conceited men condemn the other till they fee the effect: all who do fo, form their opinions on theoretical principles, on a fubject which can only be determined by fact from experience. Of governments purely fimple, judgment may be formed; but of new complex governments, of which we have had no experience, intemperance and folly alone would affume the wifdom of deciding and contemning. An ariftocracy is generally confidered by politicians as a vicious form of government; yet ariftocracy properly blended and tempered with limited monarchy and democracy* are the conflituent parts of

our

* In what is above advanced concerning the Englifh form of government, I rather complied with common opinion than adhered to my own, I fhould otherwife have faid that the component parts of this mixed form of government are limited monarchy, an ariftocracy, and a timocracy. I cannot think myfelf juftified in this deviation from received opinions without giving my reafons. A part of what is termed democratic are the members of the Houfe of Commons, yet no one of thofe is intitled to a feat in that Houfe who is not poffeffed of land to a certain annual value, and this is purely timocratic;

thofe

our form of Government. In a potion compounded of various ingredients one or more of them may be poisonous and deleterious, yet the whole medicine so compounded may neverthelefs be salubrious, or one medicine may be so counteracted by another

those who elect a part of these members must be possessed of a *freehold* to a certain annual value, or which pays not lefs than a certain annual tax, this again is purely timocratic; they who elect the remaining part either derive their right from certain specified servitudes, and this is not democratic, or, are intitled to it from being inhabitants of particular descriptions in corporate towns, and this is not democratic; while by far the greater number of the people, such as mechanics in towns and villages and all the peasantry who have not served a proper share of servitude under freedmen, or have no freeholds to a certain annual amount, are totally excluded from enjoying any share in government, all of whom in a democracy would partake of it. This part then of our government usually termed democratic, for these reasons appears to me to be timocratic.

The whole taken together produces a form of government which on a comparison with others is esteemed good; but I presume far from perfect while the greater number of the people are totally excluded from any share in government; and it may be found very difficult hereafter even to preserve it in its original state however imperfect; for if even the aristocratic and timocratic bodies should become corrupt and resign their legislative power to the will of ministry, then would the executive and legislative power be vested in the same hands, and the government would become despotic, retaining the forms only of a mixed form of government.—Whether or not it be just to exclude the major part of the people from all share in government in this *democracy*, I say not, but it may be a subject not to be slighted by ministry.

another as when mixed to produce falutary effects: thus, though the form of government eftablifhed in France fhould have one of its component parts vicious abftractedly, I fay, fhould this be the cafe, not that I know or imagine it is, yet by the combination it may prove an excellent form of government, and replete with all that is requifite to produce public happinefs. This, I fay, *may* be the effect; I do not affert; nor would be fo confident as thofe who arraign thefe legiflators, their laws, their abilities, and what they have already organized, in terms which would excite in me a concious degradation by expofing to contempt my prefumption and weaknefs in the deciding on a fubject which time and experience only can determine. Forms of government, the judicial alone excepted and which was known only to the Jews, are of human invention, the archetype has been fuppofed to be that of private families *, be this as it may, civil government has been made to involve in it the moft abftrufe, profound, and confumate knowledge; the combinations are almoft infinite;

* See Ariftotle's Ethics, lib. viii. cap. 10. Ονόματα δ' αυτων και οίς παραδείγματα λάβοι τις αν και ε ταις οικίαις; and he afterwards, agreeably to this notion, compares the timocracy to a family of brothers. αδελφική ὁ οίαν η των αδελφων.

finite; the tempers, the paffions, the interefts of mankind numerous and difcordant; to reconcile, foften, and blend all this heterogenious matter into one confiftent, uniform, and beneficial fyftem or whole, from whence fupreme good fhall be derived to all, is an undertaking replete with the moft ardent difficulties. Thefe increafe when no archetype prefents itfelf, and in this predicament are the French legiflators; for though their timocracy is extremely analogous to our own, yet the ariftocratic form is totally excluded from their government; nor could it be introduced with any degree of fafety; for though the form of government previous to the Revolution was defpotic, yet in thefe nobles the people found almoft as many petty tyrants; their *hauteur*, their extorfions and feverity had rendered them odious to the people, and their difpofitions dangerous to freedom, fo that they could not be introduced with fafety to form a diftinct clafs in their new form of government. Their exclufion by which their form of government becomes different from ours, renders it alfo a new form of government; but I have no conception that any man fo far from ridiculing what has been done, can determine with any degree of precifion concerning its inefficacy. A government fo formed may be

bad,

bad, it may be a compound of good and bad, or it may be far superior to any yet experienced; but Mr. B. with all his philosophy and politics, with all his experience and knowledge, with all his meditations, reveries, and unremitting researches into men and things, will never be able to persuade me that he can form a more decisive opinion concerning the event than the generality of mankind. The so much boasted wisdom of man, so much applauded by man, and therefore no doubt impartial, what is it at best but plausible conjecture; and generally, removed but a few degrees from stark folly. Socrates who was very conversant in governments and their administration, and has left us two treatises expresly on these subjects, ingenuously confesses that so weak is his wisdom that he was unable to determine whether the treatise he was then writing would have any claim to merit; and that such doubts were very common to authors of every kind, who though they had laboured to rise to the dignity of their subject, yet whether they had properly acquitted themselves was uncertain till it was decided by public determination *. If it was beyond the
stretch

---

* Καθ᾽ α δι επιτηδευματων ων χρη στοχαζεσθαι, και περι ας διατριβειν, ηυ πιραζομαι διελθειν. Ει μεν ουν εσται το εμον εξ-

stretch of the wisdom of such writers to determine with any precision on so trifling a matter as a small treatise, till it had undergone the examination of friends and had received the judgment of the public, I humbly conceive it is not within the range of Mr. B.'s knowledge, nor that of any other person, to decide on the merit and effect of this new form of government and the new code of laws yet in embryo; subjects far more abstruse from their nature, and requiring a larger portion of wisdom in proportion as the object is of more importance and magnitude than most others. But though the wisdom of man is, yet his presumption is not, limited. One of the wisest of his own species deriding his wisdom, says, it is something little better than nothing, ἀνθρωπινη σοφια ολιγου τινος αξια εστι και ουδενος*. And the divine oracles frequently speak of man with all his collected wisdom as a conceited fool, unable to conduct himself, or to judge properly even in common occurrences.

εξεργασθεν αξιον τις υποδειξων, χαλεπον απο της αρχης συνιδειν. Πολλα γαρ και των εμμετρων ποιηματων, και των καταλογαδην συγγραμματων, ετι μεν εν ταις διανοιαις, οντα των συντιθετων, μεγαλας προσδοκιας παρεσχεν επιτελεσθεντα δε, και τοις αλλοις υποδειχθεντα, πολυ καταδεεστεραν την δοξαν της ελπιδος ελαβεν.

Isocrat. ad Nicoc. p. 38.

* Socrat. Apol. Sect. 9. p. 73.

Proofs

Proofs of these assertions must strike every one who attends to the perpetual debates in certain assemblies, whose members unquestionably possess as much wisdom as is allotted to humanity, who, notwithstanding are almost constantly divided in their opinions on all questions of importance and difficult solution. The like too may be observed in most authors treating on the same subject, for their opinions are various. This I say could not happen if human wisdom were not precisely under the alleged predicament.

If from these legislative assemblies we go into our higher courts of law, where, if this wisdom existed, we might reasonably expect to see it assembled; yet here varying opinions are professed, uncertainty is firmly rooted, and doubts are started which these courts ingenuously declare they cannot resolve, the contested points are referred to the judgment of the twelve superior sages of the law, who are frequently divided in their opinions, and at length the determination is settled by counting of noses.

I am very far from endeavouring to convey the least reflection on any of the parties, I well know these consequences are inevitable; but I

adduce

adduce fuch inftances merely to prove, that when man extols his wifdom, he only boafts of his weaknefs; for if the legiflators who promulgated thofe laws fo framed them, that they were unintelligible, or doubtful in their meaning, this is no mark of their wifdom; if clear and intelligible, and yet the fages of the law do not comprehend them, then here again wifdom has nothing to boaft; a deficiency muft be fomewhere, or every where, and our greateft wifdom will be, to acknowledge that human and divine oracles, which have ridiculed our high claims and prefumption, are well founded, that we acquiefce in the fentence, and humbly fubmit to it, while fuch ftrong marks of human imbecility confront us, and might rifk the danger of derifion, were we to attempt a competition with the little chirping linnet, in the forming of a neft, wherein to breed her young.

To come nearer home, I mean to every man's own breaft, experience, I prefume, has convinced him, if he has ever engaged in any undertaking of confequence, either in art or fcience, that both in the defign and progrefs of the work, he has repeatedly changed his mind, and altered his original mode of profecuting his views, has made corrections, additions, fub-

C   tractions,

tractions, and a variety of alterations of one kind or another, such as his mind did not suggest to him in the formation of his original plan. But this is not the characteristic of wisdom which designs perfectly, admits of no variation, and executes completely.

But to relinquish individuals, have we not observed two distinct legislative bodies of men, and in my estimation, possessing as much wisdom as any assembly of men existing, with the executive power at their head, repealing laws which they had before enacted, or altering, new-framing, retrenching, or adding to them on account of their imperfection, insufficiency, and of their being, in one or more respects, inadequate to the end proposed, and all this laboured circumspection at last totally frustrated and defeated; and this, surely not because they possessed a wisdom equal to the execution of their views, or that could inform them if those views could be executed, but because they were deficient in wisdom, which would have directed them to refrain from, or securely to have attained the end proposed. If these persons, high in estimation for their abilities, could not frame such laws without error, I presume the body of French legislators, who are forming a whole

new

new code of laws for a great, rich, commercial, and spirited nation, are intitled, not to most malignant sneers and sarcastic coarse appellations, if they are supposed to have erred, but to the greatest indulgence, support, and assistance in their patriotic endeavours; while those who presume on their own weak abilities, and give the reigns to such licence, would have acted more prudently in examining what has passed nearer home in concerns much less difficult, lest such sarcasms, by reverberation, should with redoubled force point there.

At the worst, if the legislators we are speaking of should have materially erred, not that I know or believe this to be the case, nor can any speculative visionary theorist prove it, being a fact which time and experience alone can reveal; but I say, supposing them to have erred in the formation of their government and some of its organizations, is this a subject for malevolent reproach? it is the work of men, and the wonder would have been, to have seen it without error; are these errors irrevocable? will they admit of no touches of emendation? are their decrees like those of the Medes and Persians, irreversible? may they neither rescind nor add? have they placed a bar to the exclusion of all future melioration and improvement which time, experience, and circumstances shall suggest, till by adopting such alterations (which has ever been the invariable practice of every tolerable government, and in none so more than in our own) it is brought to the zenith of improvement and perfection? They certainly have not; if therefore they have erred, the avenues are open to amendment; what is it the most peevish or splenetic can require more? and if the means of improvement are to be found in the powers of human nature, I trust too they have abilities to discover, and the ingenuousness to employ them, having already given an ample earnest of their consummate philanthropy, in their noble efforts to redeem a nation from the two-fold bondage of superstition and slavery.

Prudence, therefore, I should have imagined would have dictated to Mr. B. if we old men could but pay half the attention to prudence which we do to our own praising, that it was derogatory to him, and indeed to any one not abforbed in the weakness and folly of age, to employ those tergiverous and unmanly terms of reproach, which at times are openly and covertly disseminated throughout his whole performance, against the greater part of the principal

pal authors of the French revolution and reform. But such reflections not only recoil on their author, they appear to me to reflect on the sense and spirit of our nation, if, when published, we do not disapprove, but sit down silently in a tame and mean acquiescence; for what a man is content to hear, he may be considered as doing, α γαρ υπομενει ακουων, ταυτα και ποιειν δοκει*. But as I choose not to be involved either in the language or censure, I here published my dissent and disapprobation of both: for were I to speak of them, I should consider each as a Proculeius, and say, in the language of Horace,

  Vivet extento Proculeius aevo,
  Notus in fratres animi paterni:
  Illum aget penna metuente solvi
   Fama superstes.

And I trust, from what I collect from my observation and the report of others, that a very considerable part of the people of this nation inclines to the like opinion, and if necessary, would avow it by their suffrages.

Prudence again, might have suggested to profound politicians, who have seen so much and meditated

* Aristot. Eth. lib. iv. c. 8. p. 186.

meditated so long on men and things, the great impropriety or weakness in assuming an authoritative tone in deciding on the event, in cases so infinitely combined, intricate and abstruse, as are the greater part of those respecting new forms of government, and new codes of laws. In forming judgment on present things, the usual method is to recur to former precedents, these investigated and compared, we draw a conclusion for the present exigency, adhering to the axiom, like causes must produce like effects. The whole of such proceeding appears to me extremely erroneous, and particularly so in the present instance. Of the precedents or examples recurred to, and the cases with which they are compared, there is not one in a million that exactly corresponds; and the least failure in the most minute article may be, and generally is, fatal: and these differences and disagreements, multifarious as they are, either from their minuteness on the one hand, or from the deficiency of accuteness in human observation on the other, escape the keenness of the most assiduous penetration. That like causes will produce like effects, is a maxim which, either through misconception of its meaning, or misapplication of it, has been productive of more false reasoning and erroneous action, than perhaps

haps any of those trite apothegms commonly bandied among mankind. All like causes will not have like effects, unless that which acts, and that which is acted upon, are in each case precisely similar. And this precision being wanting in innumerable instances where it is supposed to exist, and where it cannot be discovered but that it doth exist in every one of these instances, like causes will produce different effects, because the thing, for example, which is acted upon is not in the same precise state and condition in the one case, as in the other; the difference here again escaping human penetration. Thus, if a tax produced a specific sum, and like causes produced like effects, the tax, when doubled, should produce double the sum of the former tax; but legislators, who have adopted this theory, have been frequently disappointed, without having been able, with all their accuteness, to discover and foresee those remote and secret obstacles which frustrated their intentions.——All such reasoning then is erroneous, but it is particularly so in the present case, for there is no precedent or example to direct us in our decisions; here is a form of government or constitution entirely new and unknown to the world before, with a new code of laws adapted to it; and I could wish these wise politicians who condemn their proceedings and determine, most

probably

probably according to their own wifhes, that the iffue muſt be fatal, would, inſtead of giving us their decifive opinions, which no man of reafon would eſtimate at more than a ſtraw, I fay, I wifh they would tell us on what principles of found reafoning they ground their confidence, on what infallible criterion they found their judgment. For my own part, I am perfuaded they have none; and that they flide along with the reſt of mankind on the flippery furface of conjecture only; that they are as wife as their neighbours who hold a contrary opinion, but not one iota wifer.

But their finances, they tell us, are totally deranged; and what of that? is it not the natural confequence of fuch a revolution? and if a perfon has the tooth-ach, it may derange him, but is does not neceſſarily follow that he muſt die of the pain. But they are miferable financiers, and underſtand nothing of the matter; improbable, incredible as this is, let us fuppofe it on the word and the wifdom of thofe who pretend to be fo much wifer, and this admitted, will any one affure us that they are fo dull a people, that they are incapable of learning from experience, what experience alone can inſtruct and inform? The former unequal and partial

taxation

taxation can no longer be continued under the prefent form of government, which profeffes to deal impartially with all its citizens; of courfe then new taxes muft be exacted, and new laws enacted, to declare what they are, and the mode of raifing them; in this very comprehenfive and intricate concern, fhould fome miftakes appear, it is no more than what every reafonable perfon would expect; prefent derangement will be fucceeded by future arrangement; time and experience, in the hands of œconomy and integrity, will adjuft the whole: in the calm of the ftate, which will fucceed this little tempeft, there will be opportunity to revife what is amifs, and to apply the needful repairs, till the whole is compleat. But no rational being can fuppofe that a few erroneous calculations, or miftaken objects of taxation, can ruin a nation. A prefent temporary, tranfient, flight diftrefs is one thing, total ruin is another; but I have no conception that a kingdom, containing twenty-five millions of induftrious, active, intelligent, and commercial inhabitants, who have caft off the yoke of defpotifm, and occupy near three hundred thoufand fquare miles of territory, chiefly fertile, can be ruined by fuch petty miftakes. If immerged for a moment in difficulties, it muft foon emerge and rife

fuperior

superior to them; the powers to effect this are at hand; they are prefent and innate, and the operation as natural as any other in nature. Were they even great, alarming, and imminent, still there is redrefs, and this without recurring to the dark magic of deep financiers, to convey the reluctant property of the nation into their own hands—the people alone can effect it; and will cheerfully do fo, if they entertain an adequate idea of the bleffings derived to them by thefe their deliverers. It is a tribute which they cannot in reafon or juftice withhold, for if Freedom could not be obtained at an eafier rate, still it would be a cheap purchafe, if the price was the laft shilling in the nation.

To affail our paffions, not to appeal to our reafon and judgment, the writer furnifhes us with lamentable pictures of private fufferings. Who, in a Revolution, does not expect to hear of fome diftrefs? who fits down to fee a tragedy reprefented, and condemns the piece becaufe there are tragical fcenes? It cannot be expected of all revolutions, that they fhould be attended with that gentle ebb and flow which accompany that of our own country, and perhaps there are thofe who would not wifh it, left they fhould become more frequent. In this French Revolution, confidering the numbers concerned, and

the

the oppofing interefts, it is almoft miraculous, that it fhould be attended with fo few which do violence to humanity. Let the reader who has leifure and patience, confult Davila's hiftory of a former attempt only at a Revolution in that kingdom; let him compare thofe fcenes of flaughter, havoc, difolation, and affaffination, which continued for years, with the evils which have attended this Revolution, and he will be aftonifhed to find, that though fo much has been effected, yet the confequent calamities, on a comparifon, do not fo much as merit attention. The former was as a ftorm, raging and durable, in which the furious conflicting powers tore up every thing, fcattered ruin around, leaving nothing behind them but the deadly traces of devaftation; the latter as a tranfient gale, of fome force but of fhort duration, which deprived the lofty trees of their leafy honours, and fhook down gracelefs fpires of bad architecture, which had been too highly elevated. This has fupplied one grand theme for oratory, and your great orators have a licence to blow the foapy fuds of trifles into tranfparent bladders of magnitude, Επειδη ἱ'οι λογοι τοιαυτην εχουσι την φυσιν, ωσθ' οιον τ' ιναι περι των αυτων εξηγησασθαι, και τα τε μεγαλα ταπεινα ποιησαι, και τοις μικροις μεγεθος προσθειναι,*, fays Ifocrates.

* Ifocrat. Pan. p. 96,-100.

At one time by heightening the teints in their reprefentations, at other times daubing them with a falfe glare of colouring, and working in a plenty of the pathos, our oratorical gentlemen expect to do wonders. But this game has been played off fo frequently upon us; the keys of our fenfibility have been fo repeatedly ftruck, and with fuch injudicious violence, that I apprehend the reft of mankind, as well as myfelf, are callous and deaf to all they fay, and pay no more attention to them than

Furius ebrius olim,
Cum Ilionam edormit, Catienis mille ducentis,
Mater te appello, Clamantibus.
Hor. lib. ii. fat. 3. v. 60.

Who does not perceive that this oratory is nothing more than the fkill of playing on the ignorance of mankind, and when duped, to lead them captive, right or wrong, to the intereft or opinion of the orator; that it is the rattle-fnake in fociety, and fafcinates to catch its prey.— With thefe notions, Mr. B. will pardon me, if in perufing his letter, I fometimes fmile where he might expect a tear, and again fhed a tear where he might expect a laugh. Not that I cannot feel for the diftrefs of a king, if the dif-tress be real, for in that case, I should be as much affected as this writer or any other; but I cannot feel for an imaginary distress, where there is none, and no cause for it exists. If the distress be real, I feel for him as a man, though not as a king, unless by virtuous actions he has stamped that character with singular merit corresponding to that dignity. Of such personages it is said, that they obtain their high office and power by the special favour of heaven; I really am not competent to decide in this matter; but if that be true, it appears to me, that when they lose them, that they lose them also by and with the consent and approbation of the same all-ruling principal, for I am certain such change cannot take place contrary to his will, nor in opposition to his eternal decrees. But such dignities and powers, considered by themselves, are mere gewgaws, and he who laments at being divested of them, if he means to lament as a man, can only lament that he is thereby deprived of the means of being more extensively beneficent; and here I sympathize with him. I profess to know little of kings and courts; from the little knowledge, however, which I have of them, it may be deemed a wonderful escape, if the former are not completely contaminated by the latter; it would be almost as miraclous for a

person

perſon to paſs through the fire unhurt, as to reſide in a court and retain his probity, if the following nervous and animated repreſentation bears a reſemblance of the originals, for in this picture we ſee collected and grouped all the meaneſt vices of human nature maſked; *Qu'on life, ſays Monteſquieu, ce que les hiſtoriens de tous les tems ont dit ſur la cour des Monarques; qu'on ſe r'appelle les converſations des hommes de tous les païs ſur le miſérable caractère des courtiſans; ce ne ſont point des choſes des ſpeculation, mais d'une triſte expérience. L'ambition dans l'oiſiveté, la baſſaſſe dans l'orgueil, le deſir de s'enrichir ſans travail, l'averſion pour la verité; la flatterie, la trahiſon, la perfidie, l'abandon de tous ſes engagements, le mépris des devoirs du citoyen, la crainte de la virtu du prince, l'eſperance de ſes foibleſſes, et plus que tout cela, le ridicule perpetuel jetté ſur la vertu, ſont, je crois, le caractère de la plúpart des courtiſans marqué dans tous les lieux et dans tous les tems. Or il eſt très mal-aiſé que les principeaux d'un etat ſoient malhonnêtes gens, et que les inferieurs ſoient gens-de-bien, que ceux là ſoient trompeurs, et que ceux-ci conſentent à n'être que dupes*.* There was not perhaps a court in Europe more ſtrongly impregnated with the baſeneſs, vice, and infamy

above

---

* Monteſquieu, Eſp. de Loix, liv. iii. ch. 5.

above described, than that of France, before the Revolution, and which, it is to be hoped, the Revolution has done away. No man of integrity can conceive himself distressed in being released and rescued from such company, or in resigning a despotic power, which gave life, soul, and energy to such iniquity. I was never guilty of flattering sovereigns, but if I am not greatly misinformed, a better intentioned man doth not exist than Louis the Sixteenth king of France. To suppose him distressed, argues a want of knowledge of his character and merit. So far from exciting our concern or sympathy, he has unequivocally demonstrated to the world, that the greatness of his soul, on the present occasion, soars far above all praise, that his magnanimity and heroism are so transcendently exalted that men lose sight of it, or will not comprehend it. He has voluntarily declared in public acts, when no necessity induced him to make such declaration, that he implicitly confides in the National Assembly, approves of the form of government they have established, and has taken an oath to support and defend it. He has wisely considered, though it militates against the creed of courtiers, that the end proposed in civil society is civil happiness, that the foundation of this is freedom, that public freedom is

founded

founded on public virtue, that public virtue can never flourish where the corrupt example of the great is vicious, and that their vices are cherished and forstered by despotism: he therefore cheerfully relinquishes this odious, illicit, and unjust power in favour of the people, that they may become virtuous, free, and happy.

Yet this is the character on which it has been endeavoured to draw down our commiseration*. I profess to look up to it with applause and admiration, *Ecce spectaculum dignum, ad quod respiciat, intentus operi suo Deus! Ecce par Deo dignum!*† This is true heroism, and if I must with Mr. B. look up to sovereigns‡ with that awful respect and veneration, it shall be to such only as possess and exert this heroism. There are two species of heroism, the specious and the genuine. The former was appropriated in barbarous ages to acts which they supposed to be virtuous. A hero was a person who was successful in battle, though the grounds on which he undertook the war were unjust; and the appellation was given indiscriminately to all who laid countries desolate, overturned cities and towns, and fertilized the land with deluges of human blood,

* P. 99. † Seneca de Divin. Prov. ‡ P. 128.

blood, proudly and defpotically trampling on the peace and rights of mankind, as it were, in contempt of human nature. But who, in thefe enlightened times and days, as we boaſt, of civilization, does not confider Alexander, and the reſt of that tribe of heroes, as objects of horror and indignation; every rational being muſt deteſt the defpotic power they affumed, the hands in which it was entruſted, and the ufe to which it was applied. But the other fpecies of heroifm, which I term genuine, is of a very different complexion; it is founded on benevolence, it confiſts in every poffible exertion in every ſtation to promote the happinefs of the whole human race. We cannot compare the characters of Alexander and Trajan without injury to the latter, and fuppreffing the feelings of humanity in our own breaſts. What are the trappings of fovereignty compared with the happinefs of millions? what is haughty defpotifm compared with filial affection? what are ſtern corrofive commands compared with voluntary obedience and cheerful refignation, if neceffity ſhould prefs, of fortune and life? The defpot ungeneroufly confoles himſelf in grafping the former; the hero of benevolence affuredly fecures to himſelf the other. The defpot, if not infenfible, has but a pitiable exiſtence amidſt false splendor, attended with suspicions, treasons, tumults, fears and alarms: the other knows no anxiety; and conscious self-approbation, the most enlivening cordial of life in sickness and in health, is ever present to invigorate his mind. To embrace this, despots might willingly resign their baubles of sceptres, relinquish their false flattering courtiers, and all the mockery and lumber of courts: both cannot be held together, and he that will be a hero must make large sacrifices, by voluntary resignation of what the folly of vanity terms great and good. This the king of France has wisely done, and adheres to it in despite of the solicitations of pretended friends and courtiers, who wish to resume their tyranny under his sanction and patronage: but he has made the better choice, by attending to the one thing needful, the prayer and prosperity of the people; and in spite of all misrepresentation, he has acted the part of true heroism. will be applauded by all the friends of mankind, and will meet with that consolation in life and in death, which he could not expect while he grasped and exercised the former powers of despotism. He may now appropriate to himself that motto which few can claim, and no despot can assume—Nil conscire sibi, nullaque palescere culpa.

Thus has Louis the Sixteenth taken the moſt ſolid ground to riſe in the annals of fame, by this honourable ſacrifice to the happineſs of his people; this will be his conſolation under every affliction to his laſt moment; and when it ſhall be ſaid of other princes, that they juſt lived and died, or, proh pudor, that they ſcattered devaſtation and ruin, the candid hiſtorian will rank him with the Antonius's and Trajans, and the reſt of thoſe princes who purſued true heroiſm through the path of beneficence, whoſe luſtre, though bright, he will eclipſe, and whoſe glories, however great, will on the compariſon, "hide their diminiſhed heads."

There are in the world thoſe who affect heroiſm, but the path they purſue leads not to it; they have neither the magnanimity nor the bounty to urge them to make the neceſſary ſacrifice; the ſublime heroic character is not to be purchaſed at a vile price, they muſt bid high who wiſh to obtain it, and bring with them their teſtimonials of temperance and ſelf-denial. In an elevated and highly exalted ſphere, I recollect but two heroes at preſent in the world, Louis the Sixteenth, who relinquiſhed his pomp and power to make his people happy, and Waſhington, who after a long and deſperate conteſt,

which

which he glorioufly maintained in fupport of the rights and liberties of his fellow-citizens, no fooner became victorious, than he retired from the head of the army he commanded, and which he might have employed to the purpofes of ambition, and content with the fole reward which felf-confcioufnefs beftows on heroic actions, fought repofe in the calm of rural retirement.

Mr. B. fpeaking of the former government of France, thinks that it was not fo very bad;* in fupport of this opinion, he lays fome ftrefs on the population of that country. Population appears to me to fettle one point, which is, that the government had not cut off, or fent into exile a great part of its inhabitants. Though the government of Perfia was highly defpotic, yet was the country full of inhabitants. Climate, diet, employment, and a thoufand other contingencies affect population in general more than government. Ifocrates makes the criterion of good government to be the wealth and wifdom of its fubjects, Σημειον ιστο και του καλως βασιλευιν ιαν τους αρχομενου ορας ευπορωτερους και σωφρονεστερους γιγνομενους δια την σου επιμελειαν†. To form our judgment from this teft, the government was bad, fince in fo deplorable

* P. 187, &. † Ifoc. ad Nicoc. p. 50.

plorable a fituation were the finances of the kingdom, that a convention of the ftates was reluctantly affembled to ward off the impending danger of a national bankruptcy. It may be afked, Did the people of France, under this government, enjoy their liberty, life, and property in as full and ample a manner, as of right they ought to do, and would have done under a juft, wife, and equal government, and to which all men are entitled, being the real purpofes for which they enter into civil fociety? To this, any man of plain fenfe can anfwer, that they neither did, nor could; the government was defpotic both in theory and practice. The Baftile was the inquifition-prifon of the civil power. Any perfon, at the nod of the king, the minifter, or any minion, or of any of their miftreffes, might be fuddenly feized, and conveyed thither, fnatched from his wife and family, innocent or guilty, and at the pleafure and caprice of him who fent him, uncondemned and even unheard, might be dragged to the torture-chamber, provided exprefsly for that purpofe, and there repeatedly undergo every torture of an inquifition; if a more favourable fate awaited him, he is conveyed to a dungeon, to remain in folitude and fullen darknefs, juft tinged with as much light as may difcover to him

him the wretchedness of his situation, and make him long for light and liberty, deprived of which, he there remains fed on a scanty allowance of mouldy bread and foul water, till these combined evils close a lingering life and miserable existence. But if a still more fortunate fate attended him, and which some enjoyed under the relentless cruelty of this government, it was to be immediately murthered on coming within the walls. Thus, while the court rioted in luxury, government let loose the reins of cruelty, *adeo nec luxuriae quidquam crudelitas, nec crudelitati luxuria obetat**.

Insurrections, revolutions, war, and whatever has a tendency to waste human blood, or to destroy the peace of society, stand foremost in the list of my aversions,

> *O pater et rex*
> *Jupiter, ut pereat positum rubigine telum,*
> *Nec quisquam noceat cupido mihi pacis* ——
> Hor. lib. ii. sat. 1. v. 42.

Yet all the sophistry of declaimers will never be able to persuade me that all the aggravated distresses, from the king to the cottage, which have been

been so pathetically lamented, were not advantageously commuted in the extirpation of this hydra of power, and the government so weak and wicked as to tolerate it; a power awfully cruel to the subject, degrading to humanity, and stamping ignominy on national character. But it is asked*, comparing this government to some old castle, or other edifice, " if the walls could " not be repaired?" no doubt any building may be repaired, the question may be, is it worth the repairing; the gutting old houses and buttressing the walls, are wretched shifts; and most who have engaged in the undertaking, if they valued convenience, safety, and elegance, have repented of the folly: if men want only a temporary retreat, and their finances are low, they must manage as they can; but this is not the case in forming governments; they are made for duration, and there are always plenty of materials; the only thing wanting, is to put them well together, upon a well concerted plan, and such as will admit of alteration and addition without injury to the edifice, in case any thing has been omitted. Corruption, despotism, and other vicious qualities had not only completely sapped the foundations of the ancient fabric, but had

* P. 50.

had rotted moſt of the materials, ſo that they became uſeleſs in their preſent form, and a new edifice was neceſſary; thus at leaſt thought the political architects of France, or they would not have removed it as a nuiſance. This was their buſineſs, and why they are not as competent to it as Mr. B. or even more ſo, I profeſs not to underſtand; and after all, he could not be intereſted in it ſo deeply, as to juſtify thoſe terms of reproach which he ſo plentifully pours forth from the vial of wrath, on the members of their national aſſembly*. But the Baſtile was not the only grievance in the old government, among others, was the deſpotic power of raiſing monies † on the ſubject at pleaſure, contrary to the known rights of the people. If I miſtake not, Mr. B. ſupported a ſimilar plea of the Americans, which terminated not only in a revolution, but in a total ſubverſion of government, and loſs of that country to Great Britain, after a conteſt, which coſt one hundred and fifty millions, and an hundred thouſand lives. And yet it is to be remembered, that even the bittereſt

---

* Pages 51, 52, 54, 55, 57, 59, 61, 85, 86, 100, &c. &c.

† In the "Addreſs to the National Aſſembly," Appendix, N° III. p. 42, it is ſaid, "It is alſo an acknowledged principle, that the French cannot be taxed without their own conſent."

tereſt enemies of America never thought of introducing among them a power like that of the Baſtile, but the deſpotic power only of taxation, a deſpotic power over property, not over life and limb: and grim as this power might be, yet was it a roſe-lipped ſeraph, compared with that other hideous demon; but under the old government, France had both to ſtruggle with; it was in faƈt a deſpotic power over life, liberty and property. A government thoroughly tainted with theſe vices, aſſuming over man a power which *he* rarely will aſſume, and which no perſon of humanity will exert, in its utmoſt limit, over beaſts, one would imagine could not be worth the patching and preſerving; and I muſt confeſs, without being in any wiſe intereſted, and only giving it as a matter of opinion, ſuch a government is better done away.

The power over life, I do not mean that capricious power we have been treating of, but a power ſolemnized by law and judicial proceedings, however cautious and merciful, is a very ſerious concern; and I ſcruple not to ſay, that no ſet of men, forming themſelves into civil ſociety can, in their compaƈt, make over that power to another, or to government. No one can convey to another a greater right or intereſt in any thing than what he himfelf poffeffes. No man has power over his own life, he has it only in truft from Heaven, the fole difpofer of life and death. Therefore, when men enter into civil fociety and compact, they cannot make over to government a power over their own lives, becaufe that is a power they never poffeffed. The conditions of fuch a compact would be null and void. I will not enquire into the generally affumed authority of governments over the lives of their fubjects; but it feems extremely clear to me, that no fuch power in man over man exifts, nor can be exercifed in any cafe, where there is not an exprefs fanction for it in the laws of GOD. The powers exercifed in all governments muft be in fubordination to the laws of God, they cannot run counter, or rife fuperior to them.

To whatever crimes the laws of God have annexed death, the civil magiftrate acts in fubordination to them, and by them is juftified when he inflicts that punifhment for thofe crimes. But to proceed a ftep further, appears to me extremely dangerous, becaufe it is in fact faying, that though the laws of God have declared what crimes fhall be punifhable with death, yet I alfo by my authority will point out other

crimes,

crimes, and accordingly inflict death on those who are guilty of them. If magistrates imagine they have such a power they would act prudently in examining with the greatest circumspection from whence they derive it. But if it be only doubtful if such a power rightfully exists in any government, yet that capricious licence usurped in France must be acknowledged on all hands to be hideous, and to defeat the very end of civil society; for all modern governments are human institutions; they are instituted by man for the benefit of man, and the benefit proposed is the general happiness. *Homo, cui felicitas in civili disciplina ordinata est, ut cujus gratia ordinata est, ut est felicitas, cujus gratia tota civilis disciplina ordinata est, et instituta tota virtutum explicatio——Semper autem finis, cui res ordinata est, ceteris omnibus finibus praestantia existit.* A government therefore so extremely vitiated as to be able to admit into it such a depravity, must be wholly contaminated; and, coute qui coute, equally merits to be destroyed and extirpated, with the foulest murtherer: for though the plague of political leprosy were most apparent in the blotches of the Bastile, yet all the other parts were affected and incurable; without such a general corruption, the sources of their finances could not have been fo effectually exhaufted and dried up.

On the articles Religion and Priefthood, though I am neither Papift nor Diffenter, Mr. B.'s fentiments and mine are by no means in unifon, or rather we differ *toto coelo*. To reply to all he has faid on thefe fubjects I conceive would be a wafte of time, few perfons ftanding in need of information, or joining in the fame opinions with him, although what he has advanced is ufherd in under the pompous patronage of WE, as though he were fupported in his opinions by the unanimous voice of the whole nation. He fays*, " I beg leave to fpeak of " our church eftablifhment which is the firft of " our prejudices, not a prejudice deftitute of " reafon, but involving in it profound and ex- " tenfive reafon." With regard to church eftablifhments in general, they might be juftifiable on the fuppofition that the magiftrate was endued with wifdom from above, to enable him unequivocally to difcriminate which is the moft perfect religious profeffion. But as in all countries, and in every country where the Chriftian religion is profeffed, mankind are divided in
their

* P. 136.

their opinions on this point, and will not be induced by gentle or harsh means to renounce their opinions and embrace any other, and as the magistrate is incompetent to decide on the question, being as blind as the rest, the consequence is, that if he establishes a religion for the people which they are to follow, the people must necessary follow a blind guide.—Religion is intimately connected with conscience, and principally respects a future state. The parties concerned are the person, his conscience and heaven. I see not how another party can intrude, so long as the person disturbs not the harmony of society. To appoint him a religion, command him to embrace it, or in case of refusal to exclude him from certain privileges in society, appears to me unreasonable, partial, and arbitrary; and this too in a case where the magistrate has no right to interfere, and in which he possesses no knowledge superior to that of those whom he affects to direct.——I shrink not from declaring openly, though I do so with concern and regret, that in my opinion, genuine practical religion is much on the decline; of theory, farcical shew, pomp, and parade, there is certainly enough, and perhaps too much, but of practice there is a great deficiency, we grasp at the shadow but relinquish the substance.—

Without

Without entering into an examination of the combined and multifarious minuter reafons for this retrograde motion, it fhall be ingenuoufly confeffed, that I look upon eftablifhments as the grand original caufe. It is here, that on examining from the higheft down to the loweft officer, excepting only the induftrious beneficed clegyman who refides on his fingle living, and the labouring curate who performs all the drudgery, that we are ftruck with perpetual examples of indolence, luxury, and pomp; we may fee them ardently purfuing every amufement, gratification, or employment but the true one, that to which they were appointed, and for which they are paid. This evil, in this modified miniftry of the gofpel, has its root in the fertile foil of eftablifhment only; if men were to pay their paftors by voluntary contribution, they would as in all other cafes, fee that they performed their duty for the pay (which is a rule that thofe who object to this reftraint immutably practife with refpect to others) and if the miniftry be beneficial to the caufe of religion, religion would be benefited by fuch miniftry: but in eftablifhment, the cafe is reverfed; and I leave the candid difinterefted public to determine from what is daily before them, whether

an

an eſtabliſhment be the mean of ſincerely promoting the true intereſts of religion. I ſcruple not therefore to avow that I am no abettor of eſtabliſhments, but ſupport that every one ſhould be left to chooſe his own religion and paſtor, and to requite him as he deſerves; and that the civil power ſhould equally and impartially protect every ſect, and puniſh only ſuch as are refractory and deſtroy the public peace. To me it is truly ludicrous to ſuppoſe that the civil power is more anxious for my preſent and future welfare than I am myſelf; on this ſuppoſition it ſhould alſo appoint me my apothecary, ſurgeon, and phyſician, as well as my prieſt.

In our church eſtabliſhment all its officers, from the Archbiſhop of Canterbury down to the curate, are as much the creatures of the civil power as the petty conſtables. They cannot alter by adding to, or omitting any part of the ſervice, they cannot introduce a prayer as from themſelves, nor otherwiſe do any thing that is not appointed, or ordered them by the civil power. Such is the opinion entertained of them by the civil power, that it will not permit them to tranſgreſs in a ſingle word from what it has preſcribed

prescribed throughout the whole service. Yet under this disadvantage, I might have said the many contingent disadvantages attendant on this restraint, we see them in their various orders move heaven and earth to get preferment, so that though it is possible, setting aside this hope, " that their hope should be full of immortality," as Mr. B. says*, yet I do not comprehend how " they should not look to the paltry pelf of the " moment,"† as this seems to be the principal, if not the sole motive for their engaging in that office: meanwhile government appears to me to resemble a person who squints, looking one way and seeing another, supporting an establishment under the appearance of religious benefit, while the true object to which it is directed is the strengthening its own power, by its numerous dependents and expectants of mitres, lordships, palaces, and the variety of honours, accompanied with rich emoluments in its gift, all which are considered as pensions or life estates; and this, if the words imply any thing, is " the con-" secration of the state, by a state religious esta-" blishment.‡" *Quàm multa isti homines vident in umbris et in lucis quae nos non videmus!* § or is he tormented with the restless spirit of novelty which

* P. 137. † P. 136. ‡ P. 137. § Cicero.

which furnishes him with ideal wings, to raise him above common conceptions,

>   ——— Tentanda via est, quâ me quosque possim
> Tollere humo; *

to soar we know not whither; for after all, as Ovid observes,

>   ——— Quid tentare nocebit? †

We are told, " They can see without pain, " or grudging an archbishop precede a duke." ‡ I hope Mr. B.'s French friend, to whom he is giving all this wonderful information, and that which follows, understands that he is speaking only of England, not Great Britain, as the kingdom of Scotland knows nothing of archbishops and bishops, and bless their stars, that they are not like asses, loaded with such inhuman burthens. As Mr. B. has not let his friend into the secret, why the people of England " can see " without pain or grudging an archbishop pre- " cede a duke," I will beg leave to do it for him; it is simply this, that they care not a fig about the matter. Whether this precedes, or that hangs upon the rump of the other, interests them no more than who danced first and last at a court

G

---

* Virg. Geor. iii. v. 9. † Ovid. Met. lib. ii. ‡ P. 154.

a court ball. I know they are too wife, and I am certain they are engaged in more important concerns, than to attend to such fooleries. But the duke, who may conceive himself more nearly interested, may also perhaps smile with a sneer of ineffable contempt at the ignorance and stupid bigotry of the age in which this etiquette was established.—The explanation is, the bishop of Rome, as pope, is both bishop and prince; by fraud and artifice on one hand, working on superstition and ignorance on the other, he exalted himself superior to all his brother princes; so the archbishop following the precedent, also raised himself paramount above all his brother peers. Neither of these precedents, it is true, is to be found in the acts of the apostles, and by some mistake or other it was omitted in the four gospels, yet certainly there is great merit in that ingenuity which supplied these defects. Yet I entertain some doubt if the laity were at this time to make a compact with the clergy, whether this and many other things would be exactly as they are. If any reformation should take place, I beg humbly to recommend, and I suppose it could be effected on Mr. B.'s interest, that as the bishops only " raised their mitred fronts in
" courts

"courts and parliaments"*, that the archbifhops, both of them, fhould have theirs adorned with a *double* mitre; his holinefs at Rome has three, though it muft be confeffed the tiara has loft fomething of its original fplendor, fince the cloud of ignorance has been diffipated, and bigotry in fome meafure expelled the world.

Mr. B.'s friend is again informed that the people of England, not the people of Scotland who are not bleffed with an archbifhop or bifhop in all their kingdom, and confequently are in a perilous and defponding ftate in civil and religious concerns for want of fuch an eftablifhment; I fay, he is informed that the people of England " can fee a bifhop of Durham, or a " bifhop of Winchefter, in poffeffion of ten thou" fand pounds a year; and cannot conceive why " it is in worfe hands, than eftates to the like " amount in the hands of this earl, or that " fquire.†" If Mr. B. does not mean to deceive his friend, as I would perfuade myfelf he does not, then the true meaning of the paffage is this: Why is not this or that bifhop as juftly entitled from his merit or office to the poffeffion of eftates to the amount of ten thoufaud pounds a year

* P. 153.   † P. 154.

year as this earl, or that fquire. Mr. B. has been very cautious and circumfpect in his terms, but if that is not the fenfe he would convey, and that he means fimply to fay without regard to contingencies, that fuch eftates are as properly difpofed of when in the hands of A. and B. as when in thofe of C. and D. then we are lofing our time in contending about nothing. But if what I have fuppofed to be, is his real meaning, then this fhadow vanifhes and we may grapple with the fubftance. Immediately preceding the paffage I have cited, Mr. B. treating of thefe fame perfons fays, " that acquired perfonal no-
" bility, which they intend always to be, and
" which often is the fruit, not the reward (for
" what can be the reward?) of learning, piety,
" and virtue." From whence we may conclude that perfonal nobility, together with immenfe eftates, are beftowed on them, if not as the reward, yet as the *fruit* of their learning, piety, and virtue. I will quarrel with no man about whether thefe are fruits or rewards, nor will they, I apprehend, fo long as they can fecure them; but if they claim under the title of learning, piety, and virtue, methinks the title fhould *always* be clear, and not *often*, and that they fhould *never* be difpofed of to a claimant under a falfe title. I have already in the beginning of this

effay

essay declared my opinion concerning human wisdom or learning, and therefore shall not repeat it here; and as to piety (of which I consider virtue as a part) I am very ready to admit with Mr. B. that it is rather a rare commodity; and commodities certainly rise in their price in proportion to their scarcity and the demand for them. But dear Mr. B. for a questionable piety, as neither you nor any man can discriminate its sincerity, would you think of granting, if not as a *reward* yet as a *fruit*, the title of nobility with an estate of ten thousand pounds a year? If piety bears such fruit botanists will be at a loss where to class it, and it must rank alone under the name of the tree of knowledge of worldly good and evil, and will soon be propagated in every part by hypocritical knaves in this our paradise of fools.—Genuine piety is no cripple, therefore does not stand in need of the crutch of nobility on one side, nor that of immense riches on the other for her support; in her journey to Heaven, these, and especially the latter, would be an impediment, an obstruction, and cause of her stumbling, if we may believe divine oracles * in preference

---

* Matt. ch. ix. v. 23.—Mark, ch. x. v. 25.— Luke, ch. xviii. v. 25.

preference to Mr. B. and what if I should doubt if genuine piety ought to accept them either as a reward or fruit! Mr. B. quotes Fenelon once if not oftener, and I will take the example; in his life of Socrates he remarks, *Auſſi Socrate avoit-il coutume de dire, qu'il ne concevoit pas comment un homme qui fairoit profeſſion d'enſeigner la vertu, pouvoit ſonger à en tirer quelque profit: comme ſi de s'acquerir un honnête homme, et de ſe faire un bon ami de ſon diſciple, n'étoit pas le plus riche avantage et le profit le plus ſolide qu'on pût retirer de ſes ſoins* **. In another place he ſays of him, *Il étoit pauvre, mais ſi content de ſa pauvreté, que, quoiqu'il ne tint qu'à lui d'être riche en acceptant les preſens que ſes amis et ſes diſciples vouloient le forcer de recevoir, il les renvoya toujours au grand deplaiſir de ſa femme, qui ne goutoit point du tout cette philoſophie* †. Yet Socrates was but a heathen with all this ſelf-denial. We are alſo acquainted with the temperance of the apoſtles, and ſome of the firſt paſtors of the primitive church. Men of underſtanding muſt ſmile at the ſophiſtry employed on ſimilar occaſions‡ when the queſtion is artfully turned on the complainant by aſking him, do not you act after the like manner? for this is

no

---

* Fenelon, Vie de Socrate, p. 121. † Fenelon, Vie de Socrate, p. 123, 124. ‡ P. 155.

no more than endeavouring to justify one thing that is wrong, by another; while the point turns fimply upon this, is the matter in queftion right or wrong, and not upon who and who acts fo and fo: and agreeably to that fophiftry when we receive inftructions from the pulpit which the inftructors themfelves do not practife, we muft " think them cheats and deceivers ";* a conclufion in which however I prefume Mr. B. will not agree.

But I am fo weak as to imagine, that when an injunction is laid by Heaven on the preachers of the gofpel, fuch injunction is to be obeyed till the law is repealed, and this without regard to time, place, or any circumftances that may arife in the world;† for if the commands of Heaven were to be made to vary with human changes, alterations and inftitutions, under this control it would be man in effect who made the law and not God. Thus on the fuppofition that more luxury were introduced into the world than was practifed at the firft preaching of the gofpel, does it follow therefore that the preacher is to be enriched and the commands of Heaven relaxed to enable him to engage in thofe luxuries

* P. 155, 156.   † P. 155.

ries which the gofpel condemns. For this muft be their fuppofition when they tell us the preacher's emoluments are to vary with the times, manners and cuftoms. There was however as much luxury in the world at the time of the firft preaching of the gofpel as there is now; Rome, Antioch, Athens, Jerufalem, Alexandra, Ephefus, and many other great and opulent cities can witnefs it ; but from all fuch corruptions the preachers were to turn afide, keeping themfelves pure and undefiled, not only on their own account, but for the fake of example to others.—That it was never intended the preachers of the gofpel fhould enrich themfelves by the gofpel, becaufe if it had fuch a provifion would have been appointed them, whereas the appointment is the reverfe ; and had it been the intention of Chrift that they fhould be enriched, fuch appointment would have been made to the Apoftles as having the beft claim not only on account of their great induftry which was indefatigable and hazardous, but alfo becaufe they preached that which at that time could not be known but by their means : whereas now in thefe kingdoms at leaft, every man may know the gofpel, if he can but read, at a very trifling expence.—That the new fangled doctrine by which fome would endeavour to perfuade us,

that

that if thefe preachers are not enriched they cannot properly carry on their miniftry from the want of a due weight with the people, which is to be obtained by that mean, is a mere mockery and prieft-craft artfully introduced to acquire them wealth, or to fupport them in the poffeffion; and if the cafe were as they reprefent it, it would be as much as to fay that Heaven on the one hand cannot propagate its gofpel without having recourfe to the trafh of pelf and other worldly means for affiftance, and on the other that the people were fo ignorant that they would neither believe nor practife the doctrines of the gofpel till they were informed of the wealth of the preacher. But fact proves the contrary of what thefe men affert, and that the minds of the multitude are not in this cafe influenced by the property of the preacher; for when Meffrs. Whitefield and Wefley entered upon the office of public preaching, they were perfons of neither fortune nor property, yet were they attended by incredible multitudes whenever they preached; it was their doctrine then (good or bad, for I pronounce nothing concerning it) and not their profperous condition in life which influenced thefe multitudes and gained them fuch numbers of warmly devoted profelytes. Thefe inftances I give from knowledge

ledge of the facts, and many more might be adduced; fo that I hope this jargon will be no more obtruded upon us to impofe on the deluded underftandings of mankind, it being evident that the preachers may promote, and effectually too the caufe of religion however moderate their revenue, even as the Apoftles did; and that it was never intended they fhould be made rich by the office, becaufe no other provifion is made for them by the gofpel* than a neceffary maintenance on voluntary contribution, which is alfo confirmed and enforced again in the writings of Paul and Peter†. But they tell us, it is degrading to gentlemen of literature to be fo fupported. I know not where they imbibe this notion, but it feems it is not degrading to be fupported by charity at the Univerfities, nor to receive fellowfhips which are but charities; and if it be degradation they may choofe whether or not they will take upon them the office, no man can force it upon them, and if they enter upon it with fuch improper and high notions they appear to me
difqualified

---

* Matthew, ch. x. v. 10.—14. Mark, ch. vi. v. 7.—11. Luke, ch. ix. v. 2—6, and ch. x. v. 3—7; and in his Acts of the Apoftles, ch. xx. v. 33.—34.

† 1 Tim. ch. iii. v. 3. 1 Tim. ch. vi. v. 8—12. Philip, ch. iv. v. 11—18.' 1 Peter, ch. v. v. 2.—3.

disqualified for it; scripture which speaks plain and without ceremony alluding to them and their service expressly says " the labourer is " worthy of his hire."* But why more degrading to them than to other gentlemen of literature and of the same profession, though not provided for by a prodigal establishment, and who are perfectly satisfied with such a dispensation? or why more degrading than to others who are of the establishment, and yet accept of voluntary contribution for additional service, which if necessary, ought to be performed as included in the establishment? Or why is it more degrading to them than it was to the primitive pastors of the church who were all supported by voluntary oblations,† when religion was incorrupt and the purity and simplicity of their manners were a shining example of temperance in all things to the rest of mankind? Or lastly, why more degrading to them than it was to the Apostles who were contented to be supported, and

---

* Luke, ch. x. v. 7. See also, 1 Tim. ch. v. v. 18.

† Dopo che Cristo N. Sigore montò al Cielo li Santi Apostoli seguireno nella Chiesa di Gierusalemme l'istesso instituto d'haver il dunaro Ecclesiastico per li due effetti sapradetti, cisè per bisogno dell' Ministri dell' Evangelio e per elemosine de Poveri : e il fondo di quito danaro era similmente le oblationi delle fedeli. Fra Paolo delle Matiere Beneficiare.

and whose life, manners and conversation one would imagine, if they do not mean to deal with duplicity by us, they would in all things endeavour to emulate. I suspect that under this allegation is concealed a fallacy; or at least that one great objection to voluntary contributions is, that their duty must be attended to, but that under establishment—what is so notorious I need not express! In the interim it may, or rather it may not be equivocal, whether if these gentlemen of literature who exclaim so loudly against voluntary contributon could be assured of raising by these means twice the sum they now receive under the establishment, all this nonsense of humiliation and degradation would not be instantly in the opinion of most of them removed, and generally acknowledged to be vox pretereaque nihil.

But to return to Mr. B. and his two bishops, " They can see," says he, " a bishop of Durham, or a bishop of Winchester, in possession " of ten thousand pounds a year; and cannot " conceive why it is in worse hands than estates " to the like amount in the hands of this earl, " or that squire.* If they cannot, I pity their ignorance;

* P. 154.

ignorance; but I deny the affertion. Becaufe it is impoffible for them to conceive that their " learning, piety and virtue" can be intitled to fuch great rewards, or can bear *fuch fruit*, while hundreds of the fame profeffion with at leaft an equal fhare of thofe accomplifhments are almoft ftarving on a comparifon with their refpective incomes.—If fuch immenfe eftates are as well difpofed of when in the hands of bifhops, as in thofe of earls or fquires, why would not all the eftates of the kingdom be equally well difpofed of if in the hands of the clergy as if in lay hands? This was once their beloved fcheme, and judge Blackftone* not only fays that they would

---

* " In deducing the hiftory of which ftatutes" (of mortmain), " it will be matter of curiofity to obferve the great addrefs " and fubtile contrivance of the ecclefiaftics in eluding from " time to time the laws in being, and the zeal with which " fucceffive parliaments have purfued them through all their " fineffes: how new remedies were ftill the parents of new " evations; till the legiflature at laft, though with difficulty, " hath obtained a decifive victory."

Blackftone's Comm. b. ii. ch. 18. p. 168.

" Not content with the ample provifion of tithes, which " the law of the land had given to the parochial clergy, they " endeavoured to grafp at the lands and inheritances of the " kingdom, and (had not legiflature withftood them) would " by this time have probably been mafters of every foot of " ground in the kingdom."

Id. b. iv. ch. 8. p. 107.

would in time have effected it, but so great were there manœuvres and consummate artifice that it called forth all the powers of government to defeat their project: an evident mark that the wisdom of that government did not conceive that those estates were as well disposed of in the hands of the church as they would be when in those of the laity.—No lands in a commercial country should be absorbed in mortmain; the hope of acquiring them is a spur to honest and active industry in contrast to drowsy sloth and oscitancy; estates when they come into the hands of the church are in irredeemable mortmain, but they pass from the hands of the earl and the squire into the hands of those who are more provident and industrious. The law has such aversion to mortmain that even it has limited entails which bears but a semblance of it to a very narrow compass.—The estates of the earl and the squire descend to them by inheritance, their ancestors acquired them by labour or industry of one kind or other, they furnished such a portion of these as was judged equivalent to so much estate or to so much specie as would purchase the estate, and the contract was carried on in an open market to which every man might have brought his industry and sold it for a valuable consideration,

and

and afterwards leave it to his heir. But their lordships do not, I presume, consider themselves heirs to their fees, nor those fees to be inheritances, but rather that they are successors to them by the appointment of the civil power. What intrigues, cabals, and exertions of influence and interest are employed to obtain them, is best known to those who gain them by such means; and though it is possible that " learn-" ing, piety, and virtue" may be considered in the disposal of them, yet I apprehend they are not always the principal consideration.— How the church came into possession of these estates will hardly bear the inquiry;* the means

---

* The reader will be well informed of the manner by which the church gained its riches, its avarice, and abuse of them, by reading Father Paul on Benefices: this cannot be explained in a few quotations, the following may give him some intimation: *La gran divotione de' principi, e popoli si come fece crescere le richezze ecclesiastiche grandamente, così eccitò nelli ministri ecclesiastici gran sete al moltiplicarli, dal qual eccesso non furono manco li beni intentionati; imperoche vedendo come la distributione de' beni ecclesiastici cadeva in gloria di Dio, e beneficio commune, concludevano, che quanto più vi fosse nella Chiesa da distribuire tanto meglio fosse: onde s'adoperavano con ogni via, e con ogni arte ad aquistarne, non avertendo, se il modo che usavano, fosse legitimo, e conducente all' equità; ma purche sortisero l'effetto, cioè, che la Chiesa aquistasse per qualunque via, le pareva traver fatto sacrificio a Dio —Così avenne nelli primi tempi dopa che la Chiesa ottenne facoltà d'acquistare*

means being the fame with thofe by which they would have poffeffed themfelves of all the lands in the kingdom, had not the wifdom of legiflature prevented them. I cannot therefore on the whole conceive but that thefe eftates are in worfe hands when in thofe of the bifhops, than when in thofe of the earl or fquire; and this, were it only the fingle plea in the concluding words of the quotation, becaufe *lafciando la cura dell' infegnare la dottrina di Chrifto, tutti fi occupavano nell' avaritia*, and if there is no employment for fuch perfons, then no fuch perfons are wanted; and if it be neceffary to give fuch immenfe rewards for learning, let them be given, but why make religion the ftalking-horfe; religion, I fay, which is a fcience in which leaft

can

d'acquiftare beni ftabili, era creduto da alcuni religiofi, che foffe fervitio di Dio privare li proprii figliuoli, e parenti per donare alle Chiefe, perilche anco non tralafciavano arte alcuna per indur le Vedove, Donzelle, et altra perfonne facili, e privare le proprie cofe per lafciare alla Chiefa: il difordine pafsò cosi prefto li termini di effer fuperato, che fù neceffitato il principe di provederei. Frà Paolo, delle Materie Benefic: p. 17—18.——With refpect to the bifhops he had before faid: *Non fi fermò però in quefto ftato il difordine, ma incominciorno li vefcovi à mancare delle folite elemofine alli poveri, e ritener per fe quello che dovea effer diftribui o, e con li beni della Chiefa communi fatti ricchi, facendo anco delle usure per accrefculi, e lafciando la cura dell' infegnare la dottrina di Chrifto, tutti fi occupavano nell' avaritia, le quali cofe S. Cipriano piange.* Frà Paolo, ut fuprà, p. 12.

can be known beyond what may be attained by a very moderate underſtanding on a diligent reading of the bible; for what ſuch cannot comprehend, the learned will only perplex with unfounded conjectures. So much of a law which is to be practiſed by all men, muſt neceſſarily be levelled to all men's capacities, and they are not to wait for the acquiſition of learning, and loſe that time which ſhould have been more uſefully employed in the performance of their duty.

But " it may be true, that ſo many dogs and " horſes are not kept by the former*." I know not what dogs or horſes theſe biſhops keep, but I take it for granted they keep as many as they like, and that they would not be reſtrained from keeping more, if they judged it convenient, on any qualms of religion. A perſon who has an eſtate for life only, if he has a family, cannot confiſtently with prudence ſquander away as much money as another who has a real eſtate of the ſame income, and which he can give to his heirs. And yet ſuch biſhops make no contemptible figure in horſes, in equipages, in their parks, and their palaces, in their

I tables

* P. 154.

tables and other luxuries, wherever the spirit of avarice is not predominant; instead of dividing part of the spoil with their humble brothers, the curates, who do all the work while they sit idle, and for which they are religiously forgotten; though their inceſſant labours, if praying and preaching to the people promote the cauſe of religion, render them more beneficial in one month, than the toils of many biſhops in many years.

" When once the commonwealth has eſta-
" bliſhed the eſtates of the church as property, it
" can, conſiſtently, hear nothing of the more or
" the leſs*." I have already obſerved that the church eſtabliſhment is a creature of the ſtate, as much ſo as the army eſtabliſhment; the ſtate judged ſuch an eſtabliſhment neceſſary, appropriated offices, and appointed officers, and whenever it ſhall judge them unneceſſary in the whole or in part, it may in part or in the whole diſſolve and diſband them juſt as it may the army, and with equal conſiſtency too, applying the expence to other purpoſes of the ſtate. Who will have the preſumption or bigotry to deny it? I may be aſked, is not then religion neceſſary

* P. 154, 155.

fary in a ftate ? Unqueftionably it is, and perhaps nothing is fo neceffary; but it does not neceffarily follow that to have a religion you muft have priefts. We have a fect among ourfelves whofe devotion, piety, and purity of manners are at leaft equal to thofe of any other fect or people, yet there is not a prieft among them : the Mahometan religion extends much farther, and embraces a greater number of devotees than the Chriftian religion, yet it is promulgated and fupported without the aid of a fingle prieft; that religion knows nothing of them, and therefore there is no religious ftrife or animofity among them, they are unanimous becaufe there are no allurements to diverfity of opinion; and the like unanimity would probably have attended the Chriftian religion, had fucceeding preachers followed the example of the apoftles, both in the reward they received and the doctrine they preached ; for they did not comment, as now, on texts of fcripture, but only preached or publifhed το ευαγγελιον, that is, "the good meffage, news," or, " tiding." which from a Saxon word we term "the gofpel," and this "good tiding," was, that Chrift was come into the world to fave all who repented and believed on him: agreeably to this fays Mark, ch. xiii. v. 10. " The " gofpel muft firft be publifhed among all na-
" tions,"

" tions," the terms employed κηρυχθηναι το ευαγγελιον, must have the construction above given, and cannot imply a comment on any part of the gospel, which was the practice of after times, and probably was the instrument which severed religion into so many divisions. But I may be thought to be wandering from my subject, which I will resume and close by observing, that wealth tends not to the benefit of religion, whether in the hands of bishops, or of the church in general, that if it is not pomp but humility which should be their boast, and that they have the least to do with human concerns of any set of men living; of this I will not bring evidence from the law of our religion, where it is constantly inculcated, lest I should be accused of fanaticism, but will cite the repeated testimony of a learned bishop, who, though deceived in some particulars, yet certainly had knowledge sufficient to inform him what was his duty and to recommend a like practice to others, which he has done in the persuasive words of eloquent Latin diction: *Illud non praeteribo, quid in secretario sedens, nunquam cathedra usus est. Nam in ecclesia nemo unquam illum sedere conspexit: sicut quendam nuper (testor dominum) non sine meo pudore vidi, sublimi solio, quasi regio tribunali, celsa fide residentem.* Sulpicii Severi, dial. ii. p. 280. —

Again

Again, the worthy bishop speaking from experience, knowledge, and the simplicity of an uncorrupt heart, says, what ought to be written in letters of gold, or rather deeply engraven on the mind of every man : *Ecclesiam auro non strui, sed potius destrui.* Sulpicii Severi, dial. ii. p. 246. *Araminium (episcopi) convenere: quibus omnibus annonas et cellaria dare imperator praeceperat. Sed id nostris, id est Aquitanis, Gallis, ac Britannis indecens visum: repudiatis fiscalibus, propriis sumptibus vivere maluerunt. Tres tantùm ex Britannia, inopia proprii, publico usi sunt, cùm oblatum à ceteris collationem respuissent: sanctius putantes fiscum gravare quàm singulos. Hoc ego Gavidium episcopum nostrum, quasi obtrectantem referre solitum audivi. Sed longè aliter fencerim: laudique attribuo episcopis, tam pauperes fuisse, ut nihil proprium haberent.* ulpicii Severi. Sacr. Hist. lib. ii. p. 162, 163. For the sake of brevity I will cite but one passage more : *Centum etiam argenti libras obtulit quas vir beatus nec respuit, nec recipit. Sed prius quàm pondus illud monasterii limen attingeret, redimendis id captivis continuò deputavit. Et cum ei suggereretur à fratribus, ut aliquid ex eo in sumptum monasterii refervaret, omnibus enim angustam esse vitam, multis deesse vestitum. Nos, inquit, ecclesia it pascat et vestiat, dummodo nihil nostris usibus quaesisse videamur.* Sul. Sev. dial. iii. p. 325.

"The people of England know how little in-
"fluence the teachers of religion are likely to
"have with the wealthy and powerful of long
"standing, and how much less with the newly
"fortunate, if they appear in a manner no way
"assorted to those with whom they must asso-
"ciate, and over whom they must even ex-
"ercise, in some cases, something like an au-
"thority.*" I would fain understand what is
this, "something like an authority," this lisp-
ing, muttering expression, like that of a froward
child who dares not speak out left it should be
understood and corrected. Mr. B. is here speaking of these scientific "teachers of religion,"
who associate with "the wealthy and powerful,"
which is true enough, though it might be as well
if they associated more with persons of an inferior degree; and over those wealthy and
powerful persons, "they must even exercise, in
"some cases, something like an authority:"
For what, and in what particulars? Is it really
an authority, or is it no authority, and where is
it to commence, and where is it to cease; all
these particulars should have been marked out
with the strictest line of precision; for it is dangerous to establish an authority, which like report,

* P. 152, 153.

port, ever goes on encreasing, trampling down whatever it stands upon, and then imperiously buffetting with its head the clouds. If these wealthy and powerful persons can but read, they may soon know more of their religion than they will practise, by reading their testaments; and this may be as eligible as learning it at secondhand from an interested teacher of religion; his authority here then, I presume, is useless, for if they will not practise their duty which they collect from reading, why should they do so when they collect it from the teacher, unless Mr. B. thinks proper to arm him with coertion, and by a coup de legerdemain convert the teacher into a confessor. But " the " people of England have discerning ears" and eyes too, and I trust will never be led back again to that old state ecclesiastical juggle.— From what we daily see some judgment may be formed of this association of the teachers of religon with the powerful and wealthy, and from what I have observed, it may by no means be generally considered as founded in religion, but in other views totally distant from it, and from which all authority is concluded, at least on the part of the teacher; and as this association is fixed on the firm rock of mutual pleasure and convenience, nothing is likely to dissolve it, but

the

the teachers presuming to "exercise; in some cafes, something like an authority."

But "what muſt they think," ſays our author, "of that body of teachers, if they ſee it in no "part above the eſtabliſhment of their do-"meſtic ſervants.*" Does it follow, that becauſe no part of that eſtabliſhment ſhould be on a level with that of domeſtic ſervants, that therefore there ſhould be biſhoprics to the enormous amount of ten thouſand pounds or more annually? Is there no wholſome medium between an annual eſtabliſhment of about forty or fifty pounds, and ten thouſand! How much ſoever this gentleman may ſooth the good people of England by flattering their diſcernment, I ſhould apprehend that they had loſt their ſenſes if they did not in this inſtance make a proper diſcrimination.—But I would aſk in my turn, what opinion mankind muſt entertain of a great part of that body of teachers, whoſe claims amount to four millions of pounds ſterling per annum, while the individuals are conſtantly exerting every nerve of intereſt to get as much of this ſum as he poſſibly can by means of rich biſhoprics, deaneries, and pluralities, leave by their rapaciouſneſs

* P. 153.

cioufnefs fuch of their brethren as have no intereſt, unfeelingly to partake without relief of an earned pittance for labour which is inferior to the eſtabliſhment even of fome of their own domeſtic fervants? I may be told in the language of Mr. B. that we who complain are " cheats and deceivers,*" for we act no better ourfelves. Were the fact true, this would be only juſtifying one bad action by another, and this is not reafoning, but encouraging vice. However *we* may act, yet thefe teachers are confeffedly a feparate body of men fet apart and paid for example. All men no doubt are commendable for fetting good examples in all things; but it is particularly incumbent on thefe men to do fo, by their office and function; they are raifed as an object to the gazing multitude, and are diſtinguiſhed from the reſt by their habit, pay, and privileges; every bad precedent has more weight coming from them, than from others, and efpecially with the lower claffes of the people who form the multitude. But I may be told, that thefe men are but human beings, fubject to the like infirmities with ourfelves. To which I anfwer, that he who cannot walk worthy of that vocation to which he has called himfelf,

* P. 156.

himself, ought to decline it: his situation places him in a different light from other men; there are many things which in a layman would be indifferent, in him obnoxious; and if such a plea were admitted, vice might under it be almost softened down into the appearance of virtue, especially in the estimation of those who may imagine that " vice loses half its evil, by " losing all its grossness,*" according to the new doctrine of morality, and which it is to be hoped, our " teachers in religion" will not enforce by " the exercise of something like an " authority," till they have re-considered their testaments, as I profess to see nothing there, nor even in ancient morality, which has the least tendency to support a position so favourable to the encouragement of every species of iniquity, by reducing it to half its enormity on the simple manœuvre of omitting grossness in the perpetration. Impressed with this notion we are no longer to be surprised, on observing its author directing his envenomed sarcasms against those who would reform flagrant abuses, telling mankind that, " These men speak broad. Their " tongue betrays them. Their language is in " the *patois* of fraud; in the cant and gibberish
" of

* P. 113.

"of hypocrisy. The people of England must think so, when these praters affect to carry back the clergy to that primitive evangelic poverty which, in spirit ought always to exist in them."* Yet if those words " poverty in spirit" mean any thing, notwithstanding the commendation, it is that very disposition which we are here condemning. It is this " poverty in spirit," for no poverty in spirit can be evangelical, the term is nonsense so applied, that excites in them that censurable avarice and rapacity to sieze on the large revenues of the church and not divide them with their poor brethren; to grasp a number of lucrative pluralities, as many as he can obtain, and appropriate them to himself alone, which were intended, as in justice they ought to be severally disposed of among as many individuals †, and this

* P. 155.

† Formerly no ecclesiastic entertained so much as an idea of having more than one benefice, it was a personal service and on that account did not admit of it, and was thought to be at least equal to any man's abilities: so far from holding many, it was not permitted them to exchange one benefice for another more lucrative. *Nelli tempi primi della Chiesa, era un santo e lodevol uso, che chi era ordinata ad'una Chiesa, mai in sua vita lasciava il carico, per haver Beneficio di maggiore rendita, ò di maggiore honore; pareva a ciascun' assai face l'ufficio suo al meglio.* Frà Paolo, delle Matiere Benefic. p. 176.

this is in contempt of their brethren in diſtreſs, of reaſon, and of juſtice. From the ſame " poverty in ſpirit" proceeds non-reſidence, ſo generally complained of; for our clergy throughout the country are become ſo learned and perſons of ſuch exquiſite taſte and feelings, that their pariſhioners whom they were appointed principally to benefit, and from whom they receive their pay, are now thought too contemptible to be aſſociated with; they therefore leave them to their fate and retire to large towns or cities, where they find a variety of more rational amuſement amidſt more poliſhed company. But if we complain of theſe and many other abuſes, from which I apprehend the nation in general is a great ſufferer, we are termed illiberal, and treated with contemptuous illiberal abuſe. Yet I think nothing can be more illiberal than the practices I have deſcribed, and perhaps nothing throughout the kingdom calls louder for a reform, even though the conſequence ſhould be of calling them back to that primitive evangelic purity and ſimplicity of life and manners, which I conceive ſhould be inſeparable from their order, in all times and in all places, whatever changes and revolutions the ſtate of ſublunary things may undergo. But I would not wiſh them to be contaminated either " with poverty " in ſpirit" or to be " poor in ſpirit," ſince

theſe

these are expressions which in our language are synonimous to "meanness of spirit;" and although the former may be supposed to be justified by a passage which may be thought analagous in Matthew, ch. v. v. 3. "Blessed are the poor in spirit," yet whoever will consider the original will see, οι πλωχοι τῳ πνευματι, does not mean to be "poor in spirit," but to be in spirit as the poor are generally represented, that is "humble and meek." And this meekness of spirit though it may be derided by the frivolous, and the possessor injured by the violent and oppressor, yet is it revered by all good men, and crowned with a blessing from the author of our religion—But to return, I may be told in alleviation of the abuses, for justification there can be none, that in most professions there are gradations, as in the army and navy, where from humble and unprofitable beginnings men rise to honourable and profitable posts. I answer that the church makes a mockery of all this; that if a man has interest he may be a layman to day of any profession, and to-morrow become clerical and enter immediately on benefices to the value of two hundred or two thousand pounds a year or more; and all this attended with as little trouble as the putting off one coat to put on another, even to the

holding

holding of pluralities*, though a perſonal office, as though a man could divide himſelf, and officiate in two places at the ſame time. The duty of a paſtor was formerly conſidered as laborious, and conſcience was thought to be concerned in entering upon and performing that office; but theſe qualms being diſſipated by abuſes which are become in a manner general, nothing more is looked to than the income, and this is conſidered merely as a life eſtate; and therefore eſpecially of late years it has been a common practice to relinquiſh profeſſions which are laborious or hazardous, and ſeek an aſylum in the church where there is more convenience, eaſe, and better pay. But I conceive it is rather hard upon the laity, that becauſe theſe men have thought proper for their own conveniency and emolument to change their coats from blue, or red, or any other colour, to black, that therefore they ſhould immediately aſſume the power of " exerciſing " ſomething like an authority" over us poor laity, and none over that order into which they were recently admitted; as though the changing

---

* In the army I believe we never hear of a captain commanding two diſtinct companies; nor in the navy of a captain being captain of two men of war at the ſame time; why? becauſe it is a perſonal ſervice, and therefore hideouſly inconſiſtent.

ing a coat or wig conveyed knowledge or power, and that thefe men were much wifer now, than when they purfued their former profeffion. Undoubtably they are as the children of this world, and the reft of their order opprobrioufly ftile them wolves leaping over the fold to run off with what they term *their* property; but this alfo convinces me that thefe too have fet their hearts full as much upon the profits which are derived from the trafic in religion, as upon religion itfelf; for certainly they would not wound them with terms of reproach, if they interfered not with their emoluments and preached for nothing.

Mr. B. obferves, " And after all, with this
" gothic and monkifh education (for fuch it is
" in the ground-work) we may put in our
" claim to as ample and as early a fhare in all
" the improvements in fcience, in arts, and in
" literature, which have illuminated and adorn-
" ed the modern world, as any other nation in
" Europe."* Be it fo, but who is *we?* For the paffage is fo managed that unlefs Mr. B.'s friend reads cautioufly he may imagine he means, we of this kingdom or of thefe kingdoms; but it is no fuch matter, for *we* means,

* P. 149.

we of the church eftablifhment, who as he expreffes himfelf at a little diftance before*, " we of the old ecclefiaftical modes and fafhions " of inftitutions," and, " we found thefe old " inftitutions, on the whole, favourable to mo-" rality and difcipline, &c."† : fo that in fact he confines all this merit to thofe of the church eftablifhment. Does not this refemble the honeft trick of robbing other men's houfes of their furniture to adorn our own ? At this rate, Scotland is but a boaft, and all of this kingdom who are not of the church eftablifhment muft be confidered as dolls and idiots, for not having contributed fo much as their mites to this mighty mafs of art and fcience. Does this proceed from vanity, folly, or what ? I will mention no names, it is invidious; but I will intreat the reader to turn his eyes towards Scotland if he can without blufhing ; and on the various bodies of diffenters of this kingdom if he can without indignation, at this exclufive and filent contempt of their abilities. But this is not the only inftance by many in which this writer *Conatus eft clariffimis rebus tenebras obducere*‡ : but the reader muft be illiterate indeed whofe difcernment cannot penetrate this mift of fophiftry.

Mr.

* P. 148.   † P. 149.   ‡ Cic. Lucull. cap. iii. p. 7.

Mr. B. may flatter himself that he has said something extremely fascinating and pleasing to the ears of the people of this kingdom in his account of liberty*, and their title to it as an inheritance†, together with its " bearing and " ensigns armorial" with its " gallery of por-" traits, its monumental inscriptions, &c. &c."

One

---

* P. 149.

† I cannot by any means be prevailed on, by any thing advanced by Mr. B. to consider my liberty in the light of an inheritance from my forefathers. For it may be said to me, you claim your liberty as an inheritance from your ancestors, but where is *their* title to it, and how came they by it? You plead indeed your Bill of Rights and Magna Charta; but these are not title deeds; they are no more than *recognitions* of rights obtained by your ancestors on a supposed prior good title; that title I question; and until you have established it, these recognitions will not take effect. So that for want of the original which is called for, and which cannot be made out, on Mr. B.'s plan, we may at last be ousted of our liberties. But if I claim my liberty on a grant from Heaven, the title is indisputable, for the appeal is to every man's reason; every ingenuous mind will acknowledge the conscioufness of it, and mankind be unanimous in the decision. To claim too under this title is certainly more honourable, than under parchment Bill of Rights and Magna Charta, which grant it as an indulgent concession, or as an act derived from present necessity and which may be contended to have been wrenched from the hands of power by the untowardness of the times. And if I mistake not a similar plea has been agitated.

One would conclude he was defcribing the folly of that weaknefs ftuck up in fome churches over the vaults of the proud ennobled dead, by the vanity of their mean heirs or fucceffors. It rather reprefents the accomplifhments of departed liberty, than of liberty in full health and vigor.—I enter not upon liberty by the flimfy title of inheritance; I found my right on a fuperior claim. It is the gift of Heaven to all mankind; he has the fame title to it that he has to life; it is a grant from the fame bounteous donor; born of flaves or free-men he brings it with him, when he comes into the world; and he cannot with juftice be deprived of it but by an act of his own. Fraud or violence may wrench it from him as it may every thing elfe; but it is ftill fraud or violence, though it be the act of a prince, and as much fo as if it were the act of a private individual; the means too which have oufted him of it, will teach him, and juftifiably too, the means of recovering it. I will not then ftand indebted to man, and his feeble and frequently wicked counfel, for my liberty; I claim it as the gracious gift of Heaven, the fole author of the boon.—This is natural liberty, and this he may reftrain and confine within narrower limits, as when man enters into a ftate of fociety he then

relinquifhes

relinquishes a part of this natural liberty for the general good of the whole society: but neither this civil liberty, nor natural liberty, nor any other liberty that I know of accords with Mr. B.'s account of it when he says " the effect of " liberty to individuals is, that they may do " what they please," because reason, conscience and the laws of God, each of them and all of them, whether in or out of society evidently suggest to each individual that he is not to murther; but civil liberty, which is the liberty I am now speaking to consists in the power which every person has of doing what he pleases provided it be not repugnant to the laws of God, nor to laws in the enacting of which he has duly participated. If he has had no share in making those laws, I do not see how those laws concern him; he lives it is true among others under laws which restrain natural liberty, but what is that law to him who has had no share in the making it, and is therefore not bound to obey it: for every man before he entered into society had an equal share of liberty, on entering into society he ought therefore to have an equal share in forming those laws by which his liberty is to be abridged. I have advanced thus much because Mr. B. observes * " I shall " only

---

* P. 83.

" only say here, in justice to that old fashioned
" constitution, under which we have long prof-
" pered, that our representation has been
" found perfectly adequate to all the purposes
" for which a representation can be desired or
" devised;" and probably he might have alleged
the same, and with equal truth, if the electors
were only one tenth of their present number.
But if those who are deprived of a voice in
enacting laws should think otherwise, and they
have as good a right to think for themselves
as Mr. B. has to think for them, and should
they take the matter up on the footing of in-
justice as they may well do, what then will his
unfounded assertion avail? can he imagine his
ipse dixit will have more consequential weight
than a fly on a broad-wheel waggon. I am well
persuaded the American war, which I think
Mr. B. condemned as well as myself, with all
its ruinous and fatal consequences to this nation,
and from which it will not, if ever, recover in
a century, was principally to be imputed to this
inadequate representation; that war had never
been entered upon had there been a just and
equal representation, for the majority of the
people opposed it, which was the cause of its
terminating so injuriously to us. I must therefore deny " that our representation has been
" found

"found perfectly adequate to all the purposes for which a representation of the people can be desired or devised;" on the contrary it appears to me to be far better calculated, together with its long parliaments, to serve the purposes and schemes of a despotic ministry, than to promote the cause and benefit of the people. How long it may be submitted to I know not; an attempt towards a melioration has been begun, and for the present seems to be relinquished, but this is no reason why it may not be again resumed, and insisted on, when the first favourable opportunity shall offer.

The present unequal representation certainly does *not* answer the purposes of the people; and may be productive of much future evil which ought to be prevented by an adequate representation. Suppose eighty persons in every hundred throughout the kingdom are not represented; and that they should say, You gentlemen are represented and have a share in legislation, therefore you must approve, and pay, these taxes; but we have no share in legislation, we neither elect nor are represented, neither do we approve of this multitude of taxes, and therefore we will not pay them. Was not a case exactly similar the cause of the American war; the Americans

Americans would not be taxed becaufe not reprefented; and this doctrine is perfectly confonant to the conftitution of England. I afk, if thefe men fhould argue thus, would they not have reafon and juftice on their fide? and how would you in confcience oblige them to the payment? The project againft America Mr. B. reprobated, how can he fupport the like here; the doctrine of taxation without reprefentation was productive of infinite mifchief; is it then to be adhered to and perpetuated here; reafon and equity are againft it, and what is more, numbers. Numbers, he may fay, as he fomewhere does, " is the law of force;" I anfwer, not neceffarily fo, it may as often be the law of right. Numbers certainly imply force, yet not merely force, but alfo reafon and right. Take promifcuoufly five hundred perfons on one hand, and fifty on the other, and it is moft probable there will be more force in the former than in the latter, it is alfo highly probable that there will be more reafon alfo: no good caufe can be affigned why the probability is not in favour of there being more wifdom among the five hundred perfons than among the fifty. Upon the whole therefore, there feems to be a neceffity for an adequate reprefentation were it only to prevent the evil we have been treating of; and

this

this not only poffible but probable evil demonftrates that the prefent reprefentation does not anfwer, as fays Mr. B. every purpofe of an adequate reprefentation. Is it then prudent to fit quietly down fatisfied with Mr. B.'s bare affertion, and wait the event?

I fhall now treat of the crown of thefe kingdoms, and examine whether it be hereditary or not: but I muft firft premife that under the prefent parliamentary reprefentation, unequal, inadequate, and unjuft as it appears to me, yet we muft fuppofe it to be a true reprefentation of all the commons of thefe kingdoms, as it is confidered as fuch in the eye of the law and fiction, whatever it may be in reality in the fcales of juftice and reafon.—When a crown is faid to be hereditary, it muft at leaft be attended with the fanction of uniformity in defcent. If there be but one precedent in the fucceffion to the contrary, however minute the deviation, the uniformity of this chain of hereditary fucceffion is as effectually deftroyed by this one link being broken as if thefe durations were many and various. And Mr. B. appears to me to be totally miftaken when he endeavours to juftify his opinion by faying " *Privilegium non tranfit in ex-*
" *emplum ;*"

"*emplum;*"* for he is not there treating of privileges, but the law of inheritance, and to which that does not apply. The like happens in modules and whatever depends on cuſtom; the cuſtom being broken, the law which was founded upon it is wholly deſtroyed and done away. The uniformity of hereditary ſucceſſion is deſtroyed by ſetting aſide the next in blood, in the male line where there is one. Of this there are ſeveral inſtances in the deſcent of the crown of England. Whenever this happened it was always effected by the voice, election, and choice of the people. Mr. B.'s own words conevince this when he ſays, " there is no perſon " ſo completely ignorant of our hiſtory, as not " to know, that the majority in parliament of " both parties were ſo little diſpoſed to any " thing reſembling that principle, that at firſt " they were determined to place the vacant " crown, not on the head of the Prince of " Orange, but on that of his wife Mary.†" That *they* firſt concluded on one thing and then determined upon another, evinces that they judged they had a right to do either, and that the crown was at their diſpoſal; this alſo appears from the fact in their crowning of the

Prince

* P. 22. † P. 73.

Prince of Orange who was *not* the heir. In crowning the Prince of Orange they to all intents and purposes *elected* him to the crown; and who are *they* who elected him, but the two houses, who, as above explained, do fully imply all the people and every individual in these kingdoms. And if this be not an election of the people, I profess not to understand what is so.—So much for the crown being elective; but they have a further right, for the people may oust the possessor by whatever right he may have obtained the possession; the precedent in James II. to go no further, establishes this right, and if there be not an absolute indefeasable right vested in the people to oust and to elect, then I protest I cannot discover how all those who have succeded James II. down to the present time are not usurpers: for if they do not found their right in the right of the people to oust and to elect, they do not appear to me to have any right. The act of James is called an abdication, as though it were a voluntary act; it was a voluntary act of the like nature with that of a prisoner who voluntarily follows from necessity; and the fact is, that James could hold the throne no longer against the opposition of the people, he therefore voluntarily fled by constraint. The true construction of which is, that he was absolutely and

and to all intents and purpofes oufted by the people. And if the people had not a right to ouft, they could have no right to elect his fucceffor, as in fuch cafe there was no vacancy, for though he abdicated, yet might he again return and take poffeffion; but that which prevented this was the exerted right of the people which oufted and excluded him and heirs for ever, by their *election* of the Prince of Orange. That by which this was effected was truly an election or choice, and not an act of parliament, for the two eftates without the third cannot make an act of parliament, and nothing is binding on the people but an act of parliament; it was therefore as I faid, a choice or election made by both houfes in behalf of all the people of thefe kingdoms who were prefent, either in their own perfons, or virtually by their reprefentatives. On the whole then I conclude from precedent, that the crown of thefe kingdoms is elective, and not hereditary; and that the people on good and fubftantial reafons may ouft or eject the poffeffor: to which laft affertion Mr. B. appears to me to affent, when with ftrict propriety he declares that " the punifhment of real tyrants is " a noble and awful act of juftice;"* for I know

but

* P. 123.

but of two ways by which such crimes can be properly and with any degree of security punished, and the mildest by far of the two, and for which reason I should certainly adopt it, is by ejection. But though the crown be elective, and the right of election resides in the people, yet it is not necessary that such right should on all occasions be exercised; nothing is easier to be conceived than that a person may possess the most full and ample right, and yet it may be imprudent to exert it, and prudent to let it lie dormant. On this principle I imagine the wisdom of the nation has tacitly acquiesced in permitting the crown to devolve by descent where no important objection appeared, thereby avoiding the excesses which might probably be attendant on such an election. And I presume the same wisdom will, should it ever become necessary, which heaven forbid, determine them not only to exert this their right of election, but also that of ejection. I am, however, very far from thinking this a trifling concern either on the part of the prince or people, yet causes may in future arise to render such measures necessary; what may be generating in the womb of time no human wisdom can explore, and therefore these rights are not to be surrendered or buried in oblivion, though lulled to rest while all is peaceful,

ful, harmonious, and beneficent; or even were that harmony in some considerable degree interrupted it might not be altogether prudent to rouse these rights from their beds of peace; there should be some violent cause to call forth such powerful effects; the symptoms of the disease should be deadly when desperation introduces these drastic applications which are to succede the use of more lenient medicines and methods which after repeated trial have been found to fail.

I have been the rather induced freely to declare my sentiments on this subject, because some timid or designing minds have considered it as a matter which should never be agitated; my opinion is different from theirs for the sake both of the prince and the people. Where rights are not known and defined, there can be no certain or settled rule of action; we are wandering by the uncertain flitting gleam of a meteor instead of clear day-light. No man not verging to bankruptcy dislikes looking into his accounts, the more flourishing his condition the more cheerfully he examines them; similar to this is the case of the people of these kingdoms; and as what we have been discoursing upon, forms one of their most important accounts, the state of of it should be scrupulously examined, fairly drawn out, and held up to public view and inspection; when thus exposed, neither party can err through ignorance, whatever he may do through intentional perverseness; and the conclusion is, that many errors will thus be avoided which from mistaken principles might tend to embarrass each. If I have a right but know not what it is, nor how far it extends, nor when it is proper to use it, or suffer it to be dormant, I might as well, or perhaps better be without it; for an improper use of it in any way might bring distress on myself or others; but when myself and all who are interested are acquainted with this right and its contingencies, nothing but an unaccountable and wilful perversion, not error or mistake, can make it the cause of injurious contention. To bring it forth therefore, to assert, explain and define it, to hint at those seasons when it may and when it should not be excited, appears to me beneficial to both parties as the surest mode of producing tranquility, peace, and harmony, by keeping each within its proper line of conduct; which, on the one side or on the other, might be erroneously transgressed or craftily eluded, while this right lay concealed in obscurity and ignorance as something too dangerous to be brought forth and handled.

But

But I repeat it, that thefe rights though unqueftionable, fhould never be exercifed but in the laft ftages of the ftate difeafe when all other remedies have been tried and found ineffectual; then only, are they to be exerted, then only is the meafure wife, and then this wifdom will be juftified of her children. But unlefs thefe rights are vefted in the people their condition muft be truly pitiable; they can be ào better than hewers of wood and drawers of water; the makers of brick without ftraw for their tafkmafters; beafts of burthen, and beafts of reproach, without the hope of meliorating their condition; Egyptian bondage ceafed, but here is a flavery without end.

Before I quit this article of the fucceffion I muft take notice of a paffage in Mr. B.'s letter where he fays, " The terms of this act bind us, " our heirs, and our pofterity, to them, their " heirs, and their pofterity;"* to which he adds, " being proteftants, to the end of time." I can but fmile to fee it enforced by the words " to the end of time," as though every act of parliament which did not exprefs the contrary, was not confidered as perpetual at the time it

was

* P. 33.

was enacted, how soon soever afterwards it might be repealed; and as though an act of parliament which declares itself to be perpetual could not be repealed by any succeeding parliament; for if one parliament has the power to enact, a succeeding parliament has an equal power, and surely may repeal. Mr. B. seems to me to confound two things in themselves perfectly distinct, an act of parliament, and a contract; now this was an act of parliament, and not a contract as that was at the union, and which cannot be avoided but by consent of the parties; whereas this being an act of parliament it may be repealed by any succeeding parliament, and therefore may not be binding as he expresses it " to the end of time."—The only provision is, they " being proteftants;" as though it were impoffible that a people could be made wretched under a proteftant prince; and by securing *that* obtained every thing. At this rate our lives, liberty and property are all sacrificed to a name; and if the people so understand it with Mr. B. I cannot see they can have reason to complain be the event what it may. But the doubt is, whether they will be prevailed on to embrace this heretical doctrine.

From

From vifions of politics let us for a moment pafs with Mr. B. to vifions of love, beauty, and enthufiaftic admiration, wrapped up in the giddy rant of rhapfody. The fire of the boy in his teens feems re-kindled in the icey veins of this old gentleman; the recollection of the rays of beauty feems at this diftance of time to impart a glow even in the winter of age, and to revive the extinguifhed flames of youth and love. But he muft be heard; and obferve with what folemnity and diffidence this important bufinefs is opened, while all the attentive world ftands mute to hear. " It is now fix-
" teen or feventeen years fince I faw the queen
" of France, then the dauphinefs at Verfailles;
" and furely never lighted on this orb, which
" fhe hardly feemed to touch, a more delight-
" ful vifion."* Reader, didft thou or did any man ever fee " a vifion" with or without wings " light on this orb ?" No. Then " furely
" never lighted on this orb a more delightful
" vifion" if none ever lighted on it before. This is adhering to truth and propriety. I would have given fomething for a peep at this paragon who after fhe lighted ftood firm on this orb " which fhe hardly feemed to touch;" who
bore

* P. 112.

bore the semblance of bone and flesh which were but visionary. Virgil's Camilla was but a lumpish she afs to her, as her lightness was the mere effect of the swiftness of her motion,

—— cursuque pedum praevertere ventus.

And after all she only

*Intactae segetis per summa volaret
Gramina; nec teneras cursu laesisset aristas
Vel mare per medium, fluctu suspensa tumenti
Ferret iter; celeres nec tingeret aequora plantas.*

But Mr. B. does not proceed to inform us of his queen

*Illam omnis tectis agrisque effusa juventus
Turbaque miratur matrum, et prospectat euntem;
Attonitis inhians animis——*

Vir. Æn. vii. v. 807—811.

No; that he saw her, loved, and admired, is sufficient; what the rest of the world thought does not merit consideration.—He goes on, " I saw her just above the horifon." Where could this be; the horifon at Versailles!—— " Decorating and cheering the elevated sphere " she just began to move in." The words " to " move in," form an elegant and harmonious close to this sentence; the writer seems to have run himself out of breath, though the panegyric is but juſt begun. Thus we go on from the turgid to the languid, following the courſe of nature, after a ſtorm ſucceeds a calm.—" Glit-" tering like the morning-ſtar, full of life, and " ſplendor, and joy." No doubt joyous enough at being releaſed from confinement to diſplay herſelf and be admired; in this there is nothing viſionary. " Oh! what a revolution!" Ay, a revolution indeed, and they have to thank Heaven for it. But is Mr. B. the man of ex-perience,[*] obſervation, and all that, to be ſur-priſed at ſuch a revolution, as though nothing ſimilar had ever happened before, while hiſto-ries teem with ſuch, and greater, revolutions; and every kingdom in its turn will furniſh the like wherever the rights of mankind are vio-lated and contemned. Had I a voice that could be heard amidſt the pomp of pride, the ardor of ambition, and the tumult of paſſions, I would exclaim as a friendly monitor, princes! to reign ſecurely, ye muſt reign in the hearts of your ſubjects.—" Little did I dream," and again ſays he, " little did I dream;" though it ſhould ſeem he is dreaming throughout the whole of this " viſion;" till ſtarting from this dream, breaks forth into, " I thought ten thou-" ſand

---

[*] P. 124. et alibi.

" sand swords must have leaped from their
" scabbards to avenge even a look that threat-
" ened her with insult." We have read of the automaton tripods of Homer,* the self-opening gate of Milton,† and to vie with these we have now the self-leaping swords of Mr. B. from their scabbards: wonderfully sublime truly; may we call this poetry or prose run mad. This new invented machinery will I suppose be adopted by the military; but I must confess myself so firm a friend to peace, that I should sooner think of rivetting them there, were it only to prevent frantic frolics similar to that adverted to by Mr. B.—" But the age of
" chivalry is gone."‡—Ay, thank Heaven and Cervantes! and it were better that all its abet-

---

* ———Τριποδας γαρ ειχοσι παντας ετευχεν,
Εσταμεναι περι τοιχον ευσταθεος μεγαροιο·
Χρυσεα δε σφ' υπο κυκλα εκαστω πυθμενι θηκεν,
Οφρα οι αυτοματοι θειον δυσαιατ' αγωνα,
Ηδ' αυτις προς δωμα νεοιατο, θαυμα ιδεσθαι.
            Hom. Iliad, (Σ) xviii. v. 373—377.

† ————————till at the gate
Of Heav'n arriv'd, the gate self open'd wide
On golden hinges turning, as by work
Divine the sov'ran architect had fram'd.
            Milton, P. L. b. v. v. 253—256

‡ P. 113.

tors were gone with it, than to have it revived: there are but two many madmen already in the world without feeking for an addition in knight-errantry, when we fhould be under the neceffity of covering the area in Moorfields as a repofitory for their diftempered brains—And here we give the finifhing ftroke to this tinfel difcription of her majefty, which in my opinion is fo far from an encomium that it neither enhances her virtues, nor does the leaft credit to its author. And the reader, who perceives the qualms of ficknefs or langour affailing him, may perhaps find a reviving cordial in what is faid on a fubject fomewhat analogous by the pen of Milton, which thus delineates the queen of the univerfe:

———————— On fhe came,
Led by her heav'nly Maker, though unfeen,
And guided by his voice, nor uninformed
Of nuptial fanctity and marriage rites:
Grace was in all her fteps, heav'n in her eye,
In ev'ry gefture dignity and love.
Parad. Loft, b. viii. v. 484—489.

Milton's judgment was too refined and accurate to bring her down, heaven knowns whence, alighting as it were a fparrow upon a dunghill, there to glitter like a potfherd. No, led by the heaven of her mind, her innate confcious virtue,

virtue, and in the modeſt confidence of the purity of her undiſſembled affection, ſhe goes forth to meet the partner of all that Heaven could give in a human form; and as ſhe moved towards him,

> Grace was in all her ſteps, Heav'n in her eye,
> In ev'ry geſture dignity and love.

Thus a tranſcendent genius by a few ſtrokes gives grandeur and dignity to his ſubject; while minor geniuſes, with all their elaborate pains, mark it with a *politeſſe,* which renders it mean, and ſometimes contemptible.

I have in my time frequently heard, and do ſtill hear* the parade of much metaphyſical jargon touching governments; and when writers have bewildered themſelves in the intricate and endleſs labyrinths of unfounded metaphyſics if they can find readers weak enough to follow them, they muſt be bewildered likewiſe. This may anſwer latent purpoſes, for it renders government an occult ſcience, and then tends to exclude all the non-initiated with them in their miſteries from entertaining any juſt idea of government as incompatible with their abilities

---

* P. 143—145. et alibi.

ties and fituation; and this ultimately clofes in paffive obedience and non-refiftance. The divine right of kings, which implies defpotifm, was formerly fo much agitated that the divine rights of men, which muft have had prior exiftence and were infinitely better founded, were almoft forgotten: the combination was that the prieft fhould fupport this fame divine right, and in return the divine right fhould fupport the prieft. But the people would be duped by neither; and this defpotifm, otherwife called divine right, at one time fo firmly maintained, becoming contemptible, was fo relaxed as to be unferviceable: hereupon politicians racked their brains to produce a fimilar effect from a different caufe. To this end they endeavour to perfuade mankind that government is a metaphyfical fcience, of courfe all men are debarred meddling with it but the adepts; as thefe are few in number, fo all but a few are excluded reafoning upon it,* and as the governing power can always command a few, their doctrine will ever be that which is pleafing to that power, and the pleafing doctrine to moft of them is abfolute power and paffive obedience. Another mode was alfo adopted, and that generally

* P. 143

nerally throughout Europe, which was, that as the preachments of the priests could not prevail, a numerous military force should be established to threaten and over awe the people. This was precisely the case in France, and, though unintentionally, confessed to be so by Mr. B. for he says, speaking of this army which with a sneer he terms "Janissaries"* which I understand to be a term of contempt, " If they are not cut off by a rebellion of their " people, they may be strangled by the very " janissaries kept for their security against all " other rebellion." We see then plainly the purpose for which such armies at so vast an expence are maintained; such is the principal view in their establishment; but a fatal consequence attends it; for as such numbers with arms in their hands become dangerous if kept in idleness, so if there is no employment for them at home they must be used abroad, and hence arise those frequent wars, or massacres among the nations of Europe. These armies thus commanding implicit obedience in their respective countries, the people so awed must be wretched; where men may not speak of government and its proceedings, ap-

prove

* P. 138.

prove or condemn, remonſtrate and reform, as their prudence regulated by occuring events and circumſtances ſhall direct, ſuch ſubjects, I ſay, are no better than ſlaves or mere machines, ſtand on the ſame level with their cattle, and are confounded by government in one general maſs. Let intereſted or impaſſioned perſons reaſon ever ſo long, with all their fucated arguments, crafty ſophiſtry, and the artifice of thowing plainneſs into perplexity, yet they will never be able to perſuade one rational man, that this was not the preciſe ſtate of the French nation previous to the revolution. Every intelligent and candid perſon in that kingdom knew it, and ſighed for redreſs; but they dreaded the army which had been the dire inſtrument of deſpotiſm and diſtreſs. That army, as by inſpiration, became at once enlightened and generous, reſented the baſeneſs of that buſineſs in which it had been employed, and with a ſpirit which will ever immortalize it, gave its ſuffrage and ſupport to the cauſe of liberty. The individuals underſtood, that before they became ſoldiers they were citizens; that the duty of a citizen is paramount to all duties next to that due to Heaven; that the firſt duty of a good citizen is to reſcue his fellow citizens from the chains of bondage, and

place

place them in the situation of men. In this, that army co-operated, and it reflects higher honour and brighter luftre on their character, than if they had gained a compleat victory over ten times their own number in battle.

But this it feems in the eftimation of Mr. B. the quondam patriot, is deferving of reprehenfion, who informs us in his ufual ftile of mifreprefentation, " Thus we have feen the King of " France fold by his foldiers for an increafe " of pay."* But if an increafe of pay had effected this, a fuper added additional pay would have brought them back again; for men who act only for pay and have no principle, are always to be biaffed by a fuperior influence of profit. Hence it appears to me, that if they received additional pay, yet the motive on which they acted was principle. When mankind act purely for profit they relinquifh principle, but when they act on principle they are not to be warped by profit. I know not experimentally the influence of pay; but thofe who do, are apt to impute more to it than thofe who are unpractifed will readily admit, judging perhaps from their own feelings and actions, which however are

* P. 133.

are not applicable to all cafes and circumftances. I would not be underftood in this to fay that Mr. B. judges from his own experience; for I will not give credit till better informed, and hardly then, of an infinuation which has been thrown out,* that he receives a penfion of one thoufand five hundred pounds a year on the Irifh eftablifhment; I have feveral infurmountable reafons to fix me in a contrary opinion.— In the firft place Mr. B. was a patriot, and patriots plead not for pay in the caufe of the people; pay and patriotifm are inconfiftent, heterogeneous; when the motive is pay all patriotifm vanifhes, we cannot ferve two mafters. Next, men of honour claim no more than their due; and I perfuade myfelf that though Mr. B. thinks that ten thoufand pounds fterling a year is not too much to pay for the piety and virtue of a bifhop, yet he conceives his own merit in any thing and in all things in which he has ferved his country cannot be eftimated at fo high a rate as one thoufand five hundred pounds a year; and that it would fhock his feelings and his modefty not only to accept it, but to have the tender of it made to him. And laftly, the infinuation comes to us in the moft queftionable fhape,

it

* See, "The Rights of Men."

it being alledged that he receives the penſion " in a fictitious name;" this, would caſt a ſhade of darkneſs on the deed, and " men love dark- " neſs rather than light, becauſe their deeds are " evil." I make no ſcruple therefore to aſſert that for my own part, I conſider this inſinuation as uncandid and malevolent, the effect of envy ſporting its detractions againſt that which it has not the virtue to emulate. But at the ſame time that I cannot believe imaginary aſſertions and baſeleſs viſions, yet can I give full credit to what Mr. B. himſelf has advanced analogious to this ſubject; and he tells us, ſpeaking of the preceding ſentiments in his letter, that " they " come from one who derives honours, diſtinc- " tions, and emoluments, but little."* He then certainly deſires them; and the terms but " little," are ſo vague and indefinite that no one can truly meaſure them but the mind of the writer. What excellent ſkill ſome men poſſeſs of expreſſing their earneſt wiſhes ſo as to be thought, and not to be thought at the ſame in- ſtant, to entertain any ſuch deſire! Too ſturdy directly to aſk, but not ſo magnanimous as to refuſe; if you will offer, we are ready to accept, whether they be honours, diſtinctions, emolu-

ments,

* P. 354.

ments, or any thing elfe ; and though we defire them but little, yet we are ready to accept a great deal, and that cheerfully and thankfully. If this be a juft conftruction of that paffage, as I truft every one will conclude it to be, we have here then a clue that will guide us through all the labyrinths of recoiling doctrines fo repeatedly and falfely given under the fignature of *We:* whilft *we* abfolutely difclaim, by far the greater part of them, and pronounce them no better than forgeries, as *we* were never confulted either in the figning or in the giving fo much as our affent to them ; but on the contrary, reprobate them with déteftation, as falfe, injudicious, erroneous, as fraught with mifchief to the caufe of religion, of civil polity, and of the public weal. Hence too it may be accounted for why he facrifices his farrago of incenfe on the altars of flattery to the king and queen of France; and why, on the other hand, he calls forth from their gloomy haunts the infernal fpirits of invective, abufe, and detraction, and lets them loofe on the heads of the principal revolutionifts, the National Affembly, the army, and in fhort the whole commonalty of the injured people of France. But I may be afked, how can he " who defires honours, diftinctions, and emo-" luments, but little," expect that defire can be

gratified

gratified by such a procedure? It has been the repeated practice of most courts of Europe, that when a foreign prince conceives himself to have been benefited by the subject of another prince, to recommend him to his own prince as an object of favour and distinction; the *politesse* of courts rarely, if ever, passes over such recommendation with indifference: and men who desire these distinctions though but little, will employ every lure to catch them. It should seem then that so far from Mr. B. receiving a pension of one thousand five hundred pounds a year on the Irish establishment under a fictitious name, that from his own words he has not as yet been gratified in his desires, nor does he desist from the pursuit though hitherto he has been disregarded, and treated with neglect:

In sober old England, once wise, as says Fame,
If men could not succeed, they relinquish'd the game:
But now we're grown wiser as some wizards think,
And the case is revers'd—in distinctions and chink.

I have hinted above that Mr. B. is guilty of misinterpretation, or misrepresentation. I will select, from among many, a few instances. But as I shall make use of Dr. Price's name, I judge it necessary to premise, that I am not a dissenter, and that I never frequented any public place of worship

worship but the church of England, though in some parts of its service to which I have insurmountable objections I do not join: that as to Dr. Price, I never saw him in my life to know him, nor had I ever any communications with him. On seeing this person so petulantly treated, or as I should conceive grossly insulted, repeatedly, and with a profusion of bitterness and ill-will in Mr. B.'s letter, I have endeavoured to obtain a just account of his character. He is represented to me as a person truly venerable for his age, for his life, and conversation; perfectly unambitious of every thing but doing good, and filling that station which he holds in life as becomes a preacher of the gospel; covets not wealth, is inoffensive, mild and gentle in his manners, to which he joins the qualities of being industrious, sensible, eloquent.—It seems from Mr. B.'s letter, for I know nothing more of it than what he retails,* that this same Dr. P. had delivered in a sermon, " Those " who dislike that mode of worship which is " prescribed by authority ought, if they can " find no worship out of the church which they " approve, to set up a separate worship for " themselves; and by doing this, and giving an
" example

* P. 15. the note.

" example of a rational and manly worſhip,
" men of weight, men of rank and literature
" may do the greateſt ſervice to ſociety and the
" world." This paſſage is highly diſpleaſing to
our profound theologian Mr. B. and therefore
in his comment, he thus repreſents it: " Dr.
" Price," ſays he, " adviſes them to improve
" upon non-conformity; and to ſet up each of
" them a ſeparate meeting-houſe, upon his own
" particular principles. It is ſomewhat remark-
" able, that this reverend divine ſhould be ſo
" earneſt to ſet up new churches, and ſo per-
" fectly indifferent concerning the doctrine
" which may be taught in them. His zeal is
" of a curious character. It is not for the pro-
" pagation of his own opinions, but of any
" opinions. It is not for the diffuſion of truth,
" but for the ſpreading of contradiction. Let
" the noble teachers but diſſent, it is no matter
" from whom or from what." But would it not
be more remarkable if a perſon poſſeſſing the
ſmalleſt abilities and the leaſt candour ſhould
thus miſconſtrue and miſrepreſent ſo plain a
paſſage. Dr. P. is conſcious he preaches under a toleration; from a ſenſe of gratitude he
is deſirous that this benefit may be extended to
all. Let all therefore who have the opportunity,
not being ſatisfied with the doctrines delivered

in

in one place refort to another more agreeable to his perfuafion. I conceive this to be dictated by the fpirit of toleration. If Dr. P. had faid, I am the only teacher of true religion, and ye are inexcufable for not attending my lectures; he would then have breathed the fpirit of arrogance mixed with intolerance, and Mr. B. if I miftake not, would have been one of the firft to condemn him. And when he fpeaks in a language totally diffimilar, Mr. B. mifreprefents and condemns. Why? Becaufe Mr. B. in the plenitude of his perverfenefs is determined he fhall be condemned. Long before I read that paffage I entertained the like fentiment with Dr. P. No human authority can have a right to bend my confcience to his religion, becaufe it cannot determine which fyftem of religion is the pureft; therefore, I fay, let every man go as his confcience directs; not for the fake of oppofition, but for confcience fake. Yet when men argue thus, Mr. B. may in his dogmatical tone tell us we are cants and hypocrites; but I would be glad to know how men who think and act otherwife can avoid not only the imputation, but the conviction, of cant and hypocrify. Mr. B. throws all this cant, fraud, and hypocrify into one fcale; as though there were none to counterbalance it

in

in the other, which would be extraordinary indeed, circumftanced as matters are, while fuch allurements are thrown out as are moft likely to deftroy all confcience in matters of religion.— If Mr. B. is charmed with thefe old gothic ftructures, let him fit there if he pleafes till he contracts a tertian; but why are others to be compelled to fit there chilling and freezing, under pain of being ftigmatized as cants and hypocrites, and thus become a facrifice to his wild extravagancies. Why are their fentiments to pafs through the torturing fires of his mifreprefentation and accounted a faccherum faturni to poifon mankind, while he is the porter to the old original warehoufe for all kinds of noftrums—while, kill or cure, the profit is immenfe.

Here follows another inftance of mifinterpretation, and wilful it muft be, for the fagacity of Mr. B. can never be fo blunted as not to perceive what all the reft of the world can clearly underftand. Dr. Price it feems had faid fomewhere, for I know no more of it than what I fee in an extract made by Mr. B. in his letter,* that "a reprefentation, chofen chiefly by the "Treafury, and a *few* thoufands of the *dregs*

* P. 82.

" of the people, who are generally paid for
" their votes." On this paſſage Mr. B. makes
the following remark: " You will ſmile here at
" the confiſtency of thoſe democratiſts, who,
" when they are not on their guard, treat the
" humbler part of the community with the
" greateſt contempt, whilſt, at the ſame time
" they pretend to make them the depoſitaries of
" all power."* Mr. B. muſt ſurely imagine
his friend to whom he addreſſes his letter to be
the verrieſt dolt that ever exiſted, to think that
he ſhould ſmile truly, while Mr. B. is impoſing
on him by miſrepreſentation. The words of
Dr. P. are to be taken together as they ſtand
connected, " the dregs of the people who are
" generally paid for their votes;" and Dr. P.
with all other democratiſts never could dream
of making this venal tribe the depoſitaries of
power, but the objects of contempt and ſevere
puniſhment, and therefore he certainly is con-
ſiſtent in thus expoſing ſuch infamous characters
to the ſcorn of mankind. In the interim I will
beg leave to ſubmit to the conſideration of Mr.
B.'s friend a remark or two much more juſt
than that of Mr. B. which is, that all democratiſts have a great and ſincere regard for the
honeſt

* P. 82.

honest and virtuous in the humbler or lower classes of the people; they know they have power, all revolutions evince it; as they have power they ought also to have some share in legislation were it merely with a view to policy, omitting justice, thereby soothing them to promote the general tranquility and preventing revolutions. In point of justice viewing them as men, they are intitled to it; in a free country can any man who has not forfeited his right be excluded from a share in legislation; it is contradiction in terms. And if we consider it with respect to taxation, here again his right is obvious; not only *they* also pay taxes, but it will be found I presume on enquiry that those in this kingdom who have no share in legislation, pay as great a part of the taxes, as those who have. And lastly, as to the article of utility, no nation can exist without them. If Mr. B. is of opinion that a government charged with this and other striking partialities can be firm, stable, and durable, I must freely confess I differ from him in opinion, and tremble for the consequences arising from these masses of leaven which are maturing with time to burst forth in some dangerous fermentation; to tell men of old constitutions, and forms and ceremonies, will then avail but little, and the wiser policy is surely to labour at improvement and melioration while yet it is day, and the subject is capable of receiving the remedies, and the rulers of applying them with success. But obstinacy is not connected with reason, nor misrepresentation with candour; and Dr. P. has not said that the commonalty of the people are corrupt and venal, but that there are a few thousands of the dregs of the people, meaning, I suppose, the voters in many of our rotten boroughs, who being generally paid for their votes, are so. But Mr. B. because he happens to be himself pure and immaculate on the article of venality (which consists partly in accepting remuneration for professions of patriotism and the verbal service to one's country) cannot possibly imagine such voters, who also voted to serve their country, would receive for that service any reward; he concludes therefore that the supposition of Dr. P. is injurious, and comes forward to defend their cause by misrepresenting what Dr. P. had advanced; and instead of giving us Dr. P.'s own words concerning the infamous bribe alluded to, converts both the terms and the persons by saying, " the *humbler* " part of the community." There are crafty jesuits in all countries, but they may be defied to exceed this manœuvre. I hope Mr. B.'s

friend

friend is not so ignorant as to be deluded by this imposition on his understanding.

I am concerned Mr. B. should have given so much reason to complain that his letter, either from inadvertence, design, want of information, or from whatever cause it proceeds, is replete with misrepresentation; it would be an endless task to collect the several instances; I shall therefore advert only to one or two more.—That there were riots and excesses committed at Versailles on the 6th of October, 1789, no one denies, nor can any person in his senses approve of them; yet to a philosophic mind great allowance might be made for an intemperate and intoxicating draught of freedom taken by the populace, while the thirst occasioned by the fever of despotism was yet upon them. That these excesses were as great as represented by Mr. B. I have some reasons to doubt;* nor was he there to prove his assertions. Improving on the report of others he forms his plaintive commiserating tale, ever partially adhering to one side of the question; whereas had he confined himself to the bare truth without embellishment, or had he explained

* P. 105.

plained the *whole* tranfaction, much might have been adduced in mitigation. But then indeed the tale would have fuffered confiderably in the pathos, for which purpofe it feems to have been principally calculated. If Mr. B. is really acquainted with the whole of that tranfaction, he will perhaps perceive that the following epitomized narration is pretty near the truth.— Some of the principals in the French revolution had received indubitable intelligence, that a plot was concerted to remove, or more properly to carry of the king from Verfailles to Metz; they had the names of the chiefs concerned in the confpiracy againft the ftate, together with a moft minute account of all the progreffive meafures that were to be taken before and after that event, by an intercepted courier to a perfon whofe name it is not neceffary here to introduce. If the king was removed as propofed, the inevitable confequence was deemed to be a civil war carried on in the king's name againft the people. The knowledge of this confpiracy was endeavoured to be concealed from the populace, and continued to be fo for fome time; while thofe who were in the fecret, employed every precaution to defeat the intended removal and confpiracy, not divulging the motive of their proceedings left coming to

the

the public ear the people should be too violently exasperated. A matter of such magnitude, and known to more than one person, would not be long hushed in silence; those who had gained the intelligence divulged it to others, these communicated it again, and the whole was known in a short time to every person in Paris. Part of the populace, perhaps to the amount of thirty thousand, frantic on this report, without knowing for what purpose, and without any concerted design immediately rushed forwards to Versailles; when they came there, having no fixed purpose, so they did nothing; the night following all was quiet. But early on the next morning the king's body-guard who conceived themselves to be watched by the populace began to be out of humour, reflected on the populace for wearing the national cockade, which was followed by other provocations, and these from the other side were resented and returned. On this, one of the king's guard fired either a pistol or a musket among the populace whereby one of them was killed. The multitude enraged, assaulted the gaurds, who again fired upon them, and an action commenced. The guards were repulsed, and retreated to the palace; the populace in their fury pursued them into the very apartments whither they

they had retreated sparing none, and cutting down every man they met.—That the populace had any the least premeditated design against the life of either the king or the queen, is a circumstance which I no more believe than I do that Mr. B. was present at the transaction; I do not even suspect that they intended either of them the least violence.—The plain unsophisticated fact, and which has been artfully worked up to serve sinister purposes by exciting commiseration and affecting the passions of mankind to prejudice the revolution, is simply this: the populace of Paris ignorantly rushed forth to Versailles under the notion of preventing the king's escape; when arrived, they behaved peaceably, till the guard imprudently fired upon them, and made themselves the aggressors; retaliation succeeded, a general action commenced, the guards overpowered retreated, the enraged victors pursued and slaughtered them in the very recesses of the palace, from which the illustrious personages had fled; inflamed with rage and vengeance for the insult received from the guards, they were determined if possible none should escape, and with their bayonets they pierced the queen's bed lest any of them should have taken refuge and concealment there.—This I trust is a plain but true

narrative

narrative of that transaction, which from such fact has been worked up into as arrant fiction as any of the tales in Ovid's Metarmorphoses. But as I imagine mankind are not likely to give credit to such fables, less occasion is there to say more concerning it. I would not however in any thing I have said he understood to applaud or even to countenance a single action in this scene of rage, even when represented with candour: much less in that picture which has been given of it. The less men are acquainted with the circumstances, the more should they avoid describing them. But in what estimation are we to hold those who are acquainted with the whole but suppress a part for the purpose of deception, and thus work it up into a tale to play upon the passions by misrepresentation for sinister views, and to cast an odium on men and measures merely because they do not quadrate with their whimsical fancies and caprices; and to do this the more effectually pass over whatever might tend to give true information, and in some measure extenuate these excesses;

Foibles amusemens d'une douleur si grande! *

Q   From

* Racine, Berenice.

From the fame manufactory of mifreprefentation we are inftructed to vilify the donations of the French nation: but before the ridicule can be fuppofed to take place, we are to be led to imagine that fuch donations were intended as a fubftitute for taxes, or at leaft to make up for their deficiency.* It appears to me that from pique nothing can be more difingenuoufly reprefented than thefe offerings of the people to the National Affembly; nothing can be more wantonly ridiculed, more petulantly derided, or more puerilely conftrued. The "fapient" Mr. B. muft furely know what all the world is acquainted with, that in all facrifices the value of the offering is not the point to be attended to, but the mind, the difpofition of him who makes the oblation which is thereby expreffed. Neither hecatombs, nor temples could enrich Heaven; and a falted cake was as acceptable, becaufe the fentiment was equally difplayed in the latter as by the former,

Non fumptuofa blandior hoftia
Mollebit averfos penates
Farre pio, et faliente mica.

Hor. Od. xvii. lib. 3.

And

* P. 57, 339, 340. et alibi.

And on this principle Horace says to Mecenas,

>   ———Reddere victimas,
> Ædemque votivam memento:
> Nos humilem feriemus agnam.
>
> Hor. Od. xvii. lib. 2.

The trinkets and trifles so eagerly brought from every quarter, if we survey them with a view to national finance, perversely turning our eyes from the donors and the disposition which accompanied them to merely the things given, might be considered as insignificant unimportant bawbles. But to look on them in this light only betrays, in my apprehension, either a weak or mischeivous habit of judging. The people indiscriminately pressed forward to make a sacrifice of such things they had at the altar of liberty in presence of the National Assembly, whom they looked up to as their deliverer from the iron arm of despotism. The proudest monarch in Europe might, and I trust would, glory in such a sacrifice. Compare these oblations, truly expressive of the feelings of the heart, with the frothy addresses where nothing of what is expressed is felt. Compare them with the fulsome flattery of courts and of lofty nobility, while it sinks into servile offices and abject compliances degrading to a private gentleman of spirit.

fpirit. Compare them with the empty proffers of life and fortune obtained by artifice and publifhed with oftentation, from perfons who never intend to move fo much as a finger in the caufe they pretend to fupport. All, crafty impofitions on monarchs, to excite in their minds vifionary and and delufive dreams, ever to their injury, and fometimes to their ruin. On a comparifon, that one is a real fubftance, the other a fhadow. In France the holy flame of freedom darted from man to man, and in an inftant like electrical fire pervaded every breaft, nor is it within the circumfcribed imagination of Mr. B. who " defires honours, diftinctions, " and emoluments" though " but little," and who feems with a ghaftly fmile to put a perverfe mifconftruction on almoft every thing that has been faid or done by thefe revolutionifts, to limit fuch a fpirit, or to fay what it will perform for the public good. Men who would not offer an atom of their property to the demon of defpotifm, may facrifice their all to the deity of freedom : while he may lie looking out to foreign courts for exotic human deities propitioufly to fmile on the oblation of his literary incenfe.

The

The confiscation of church property in France seems also to hurt Mr. B. much; but I who have nothing to hope or fear from any man, and am totally uninfluenced, will freely speak my mind on this business; and ingenuously confess that the mode by which that property was acquired by the clergy, hurts me much more than their loss of it. In the acquisition, increase, detention, and disposal of it there was scarcely any species of art, artifice, and fraud that was left unpractised. To enrich the church, the timorous and weak in understanding among the laity, were as palpably and completely duped out of their property as they could be by any set of swindlers whatever. The priests were indefatigable in their pursuit of wealth, which they obtained from every quarter and by every mean. When princes were distressed and too feeble to resist, they bullied them out of their lands and forcibly kept possession; when powerful, they gained their ends by flattery and adulation. They robbed the poor of the fund with which they were entrusted for their support, and for preserving the edifices of devotion which they left to fall into ruin, applying the money to their own avaricious or luxurious purposes. And in short, hardly any method was left unattempted by which they might arrive at wealth and power.

It

It may be said these are heavy charges. I answer, they are no more weighty than they are true; neither are they mine; they come from unquestionable authority. It is impossible for me in this place to go through the whole of this history; but I will epitomize so much of it as is necessary for my purpose and produce my voucher.

At the commencement of Christiany and so early as the times of the apostles, the preachers and the poor were supported by oblations, alms, and voluntary contributions of the faithful, which formed one stock to supply their respective necessities.* These contributions in a short time became great from a prevalent opinion among Christians at that time, that a dissolution of the world was at no great distance, and of course their property could not be better bestowed

---

* *Doppo che Christo nostro Signore montò al Cielo li Santi Apostoli seguirono nella chiesa di Gierusalemme l'istesso instituto d'haver il danoro ecclesiastico per li due effetti sopradetti, cioè per bisogno delli ministri dell' Evangelio e per elemosine die poveri: e il fondo di questo danoro era similmente le oblationi delli fedeli, quali anco mettendo ogni loro haver in commune.*

F. Paoli Sarpi, delle Mat. Beneficiare, p. 6.

flowed than in alms.* As by such liberal contribution the church was enriched, the bishops or pastors of the flock were no longer satisfied with remaining on their former footing, would live no longer in common, but separated, took a house for themselves, and had their allowance paid in money.† But the disorder did not close here, for they began to withhold from the poor their share of the alms, and to apply it fraudulently to their own use; laid out their money on usury; and wholly neglecting the duties of their function, devoted themselves to avarice.‡ As

avarice

* *Erano molto pronti li christiani in quei primi tempi à spogliarsi delli beni temporali per impiegarli in elemosine, perche aspettavano di prossimo il fine del mondo travendoli Christo N. Signore lasciati in incerti, e quantenque fosse per durare quanto si volesse, non l'haveano per considerabile più, che se fosse all' hora per finire, tenendo per fermo, che la figura di questo mondo, cioè lo stato della vita presenti trapassa; perche ancor le oblationi sempre più s'aumentavano.* Id. ib. p. 6—7.

† *Doppo che le chiesa furono fatte ricche, anco li clerichi cominciorono à vivere con maggior commodità, e alcuni non si contentando di quel vitto commune della chiesa quotidiano, volsero vivere separatamente nella propria casa, e dalla chiesa haver la sua portione separatamente in danari igni giorno ò per un mese continuo, e ancora per il più lungo tempo.* Id. ib. p. 12.

‡ *Non si fermò però in questo stato il disordine, ma incominciorno li vescovi à mancare delle solite elemosine alli poveri, e ritener per*

se

avarice has no bounds, they perfevered in the fpirit of accumulation, and from weak princes beguiled with the idea of devotion they now obtained permiffion to poffefs real eftates.* From this period avarice raged with thefe wretches, and every engine of art and artifice with complicated fraud was worked to enable them to feize on every fpecies of property; the weak of all conditions and ranks, but principally widows and maidens, became their prey; by gift or teftament the relation, the heir, and the orphan were fwindled out of their inheritance; it was transferred to the church, which with infatiate hunger like the grave fwallowed all, and ftill gaped

fe quello che dovea effer diftribuito, e con li beni della chiefa communi fatti ricchi, faccendo anche delle ufure per aurefculi, e lafciando la cura dell' infignare la dottrina di Chrifto, tutti fi occupavano nell' avaritia. Id. ib. p. 12.

* *Maffentio otto anni doppo reftitui tutte le poffeffioni alla chiefa Romana, e poco doppo Conftantino; e licinio conceffa la liberta di religione alli chriftiani, e approvati li collegii ecclefiaftici, che con voce Greca chiamavano chiefe, conceffe generalmente per tutto l'imperio, che poteffero acquefiare beni ftabili cosi per donation, come per teftamento, efentando ancora li clerichi dalle fattioni perfonali publiche, acciò poteffero attendere più commodamente al fervitis della religione.* Id. ib. p. 14—15.

gaped for more.* The flagrancy of these iniquitous practices alarmed mankind, they had proceeded to so great a length as to be almost past redress; an edict came forth to repress and control them: but without effect.† And this was succeeded by another which absolutely forbade widows devoting themselves to the church from giving or bequeathing to it any moveables or immoveables of any value.‡ But neither these repressive edicts, nor any remonstrances could prevail on ecclesiastics from enriching themselves beyond

the

---

* *Così avenne nelli primi tempi doppo che la chiesa ottenue facoltà d'acquistare beni stabili, era creduto d'alcuni religiosi, che fosse servitio di dio privare li proprii figliuoli, a parenti per donare alle chiese, perilche non tralasciavano arte alcuna per indur le Vedove, Donzelle, ed altre persone facili à privare le proprie case per lasciar alla chiesa.* Id. ib. p. 18.

† *Il disordine passò così presto li termini desser superato, che fù necessitato il principe di provederci, e del 370 fù fatta la legge che se ben non privava le chiese d'acquistare assolutamente, prohibiva però a gle ecclesiastici l'andar in casa di Vedove, e pupilli, e il recevere per donatione, ò testamenta alcuna cose dalle donne, non solo direttamente, ma ne anco per mezo di terza persona; la qual legge S. Girolamo, confessa esser stata medicina per la corruttione entrata nelli clerici.* Id. ib. p. 18.

‡ *Pace anni dopo, cioè dell 390 fù fatto un' altra legge, che la Vedova, quale si dedicava alli servitii della chiesa non potesse donargli, o lasciargli per testamento beni stabili, ò mobili pretiosi di casa.* Id. ib. p. 19.

the bounds of all reafon.* Poffeffing great opulence and power they interfered in what did not concern them; they not only traded, and were exempted from all duties; † but on a rebellion of cities againſt the emperor they headed them, and feized on the rights and royalties of the crown, which they would never relinquiſh, fo that in the concluſion they remained with them as fiefs, whence feveral of the biſhops derive their titles,‡ which they maintain to this day;

* *Ma con tutti i freni poſti dalli Santi Padri con le buone efortationi, e delli Principi con le buone leggi, non ſi potè però fare che li beni ecclefiaſtici non ereſceſſero foprà il dovere.* Id. ib. p. 20.

† *Ritrovaſi nel Codice Theodoſiano una legge di conſtanto de* 359 *che eſenta lillerici mufanti dal pagar dazio.* Id. ib. p. 23.

‡ *Nelle turbe, che ſucceſſero per le cauſe ſudette molte città ſolevate dalli Veſcovi confederati col Papa ſi ribellorono dall' Imperatore, e li Veſcovi ſe ne fecero Capi, onde ottenero anco le publiche entrate, e le ragioni regie; e quando le differenze ſi compoſero haveano preſo coſi fermo poſſeſſo, che fù neceſſitato il Prencipe conceder Coro in feudo quelle, che de facto ſi erano uſurpato, onde anche acquiſtorno li titoli di Duchi, Marcheſi, Conti, come molti ne ſono in Germania, che reſtano anco tali, & in nome, & in fatti, ed in Italia di nome ſolo, il che fece ecclefiaſtici gran quantità di beni feclari e fù aumento molto notabile, non ſolo nelle turbe di che habbiamo parlato, mà in quelle ancora, che feguirono ſotto gl' Imperatori Suevi.* Id. ib. p. 102, 103.——Nor is what is advanced confined to Germany alone; the like took place in France, and it was purely on account of theſe fiefs that the French biſhops were obliged to attend in the holy wars as they are called.

day; for according to the practice of all invaders and usurpers, they set up long possession in opposition to a right and just title; *missum disceptatorem a Claudio agrorum, quos regis Apionis quondam habitos, et populo Romano cum regno relictos, proximus quisque possessor invaserant diuternaque licentia et injuria, quasi jure et aequo, nitebantur;** so that in fact they were obtained and maintained by violence and fraud.

Possessing such wealth, without considering at this moment by what means it was acquired, I am not in the least surprized when I am informed that the necessitous heathen emperors occasionally laid their fingers on church treasures; and this the rather if they vouchsafed themselves, or any one for them, to look into the New Testament, where they could not fail of observing that the author of the Christian religion renounces all claim to the wealth† of this world, expressly informs the preachers of his gospel, that they are to claim no more of this world than is expedient to supply their necessities;

---

* Tacit. Ann. lib. xiv. sect. 18.

† My kingdom is not of this world. John, ch. xviii. ver. 56; and to the same effect in many other passages of the gospels.

cessities;* that some of the† apostles in their epistles to the pastors remind them of the same doctrine, and that being supplied with these necessaries they are to be therewith content. The heathen emperors therefore on seeing a doctrine so plain, clear, and express, thus scandalously transgressed by these ecclesiastics, would consider them in no better light than a set of deceivers, and therefore proper object of plunder and punishment. If ye will adhere, might they say, to the laws of the religion ye profess, go on unmolested, for we discover nothing in it that counteracts our authority; it will render you modest and humble men, the friends of morality, virtue, and temperance. But ye have thrown aside your law, far exceeded all the limits prescribed you by your religion, and grossly violated the commands of its author, which indicates that ye have either no belief, or

no

* Luke, ch. x. ver. 7, 8.

† And having food and raiment let us be therewith content. But they that will be rich fall into temptation, and a snare, and into many foolish and hurtful lusts, which drown men in destruction and perdition. For the love of money is the root of all evil.—But thou, O man of God, flee these things and follow after righteousness, godliness, faith, love, patience, meekness. Paul, 1 Tim. ch. vi. ver. 8, &c. And to the same purpose in innumerable passages of the Testament.

no principle; and as there is no human power that can or will reprefs this licence, we will make your crimes fubfervient to our neceffities, and for punifhment will take from you that which by the law of your religion you have no right to acquire or poffefs.* I cannot therefore blame the emperor Decius, whatever ecclefiaftics may do, for fending an officer to St. Lawrence, as he is called, a fuperintendent of church treafures, with the meffage: Quod Cæfaris fcis Cæfari da, nempe juftum poftulo; ni fallor, haud ullam tuus fignal Deus pecuniam.† The true meaning of which is, " Your church hath " amaffed great riches which by the law of your " religion you cannot poffefs, therefore refign " them, to Cæfar who may poffefs and now " wants them; your lawgiver laid no claim to
" fuch

---

* An emperor, though a heathen, who fhould reafon after this manner, would not exprefs himfelf very differently from what St. Ciprian is reported to have faid: *Con li beni della chiefa fatti ricchi, facendo ancor delle ufere per accrefcerli, e lafciando la cura dell' infegnare la dottrina di Crifto, tutti fi occupavano nell' avaritia, le quale cofe S. Cipriano piange, che nel fuo tempo foffero ufate, e conclude, che per purgare la fua chiefa da quefti errori Dio pumeteffe quella gran perfecutione.*

F. Paolo Sarpi, delle M. Benef. p. 12.

† That is, " What you know to be Cæfar's give to Cæfar; " I afk no more than is juft, for if I miftake not, your God " coins no money." This is recorded by Prudentius.

"such things nor suffered you to do so, but said, render unto Cæsar the things which are Cæsar's, and unto God the things which are God's, that is, your devotions, and meddle not with what does not concern you."*—Where is the impropriety of it? That wealth, provided he were a good emperor, was certainly better deposited in his hands for the benefit of the state, than to remain the treasure of ecclesiastics, contrary to religion, and probably to be employed to pernicious purposes.

I may be told in the reasoning of Mr. B. that supposing all to be true which has been advanced concerning the quantity of this wealth, and the mode of acquiring it, yet those persons in France, who on the Revolution are dispossessed, are not the persons who committed these artifices and frauds. True, but they are the successors of those who so possessed themselves of that property; and the successors of those who

---

* It is observable, that at these times the church was always very charitable; for it no sooner had intimation of these designs, than it distributed largely to the poor, lest their wealth should fall into the hands of the emperors. When they could no longer keep it, they recollected where it ought to have gone; but so long as they could grasp it, their memory failed them.

who were so duped now recover them from those unjust possessors. Possession is not right, and it is the constant practice, as I have above observed, for invaders and usurpers to set up a long unjust possession in opposition to a just claim and title. What is obtained by fraud or force is always in justice recoverable; and no man or set of men are to be benefited by their iniquity, nor ought their successors to reap the advantage.

But even supposing this property had not been obtained by indirect means, yet I see no reason why the nation might not dispossess them. It had hitherto been appropriated to particular persons for particular purposes in the nature of a salary, but which was rather converted into pension; and if such men and such purposes were no longer necessary, or if only a certain number of them were deemed expedient, the state had a right to discharge the remainder, and to apply the residue of such salary or pension to the public necessity. Is a state under obligation to keep up all its old forms, appointments, ceremonies, when they become useless, injurious, or too expensive? If so, the admission of any pension becomes extremely dangerous, for when once granted it must remain

main a burthen on the people for ever; and on this principle I do not fee how our anceftors could be juftified in changing the religion of the country and making it proteftant, for not only doctrines, but appointments, forms, ceremonies, and old eftablifhments were totally reverfed or fuperfeded. In fhort, fuch quaint reafoning carried to its extent would preclude all improvement of every kind in every ftate.

Before a religious or church eftablifhment in any ftate can be pleaded, it might firft be proper to fhow that fuch men are abfolutely neceffary to promote religion, and that religion cannot be duly promoted without them. This point which by fome means or other is generally taken for granted, I cannot admit till it has been properly difcuffed. In our own country as I have before obferved, we have a religious fect among whom are no priefts; yet I prefume no perfon of candour will fay, that in point of moral and religious principles, which are to be determined by their effect, that is, by life and converfation, that thefe perfons are inferior to thofe of any eftablifhment whatever. This admitted, for I truft it cannot be denied, here then is an inftance to prove that priefts are not abfolutely neceffary to promote religion,

gion, and that religion may be properly promoted without priefts.—At firft and originally I grant this might not be the cafe; but when once the gofpels were written and difperfed, I do not fee that thefe men became any longer abfolutely neceffary. Perhaps it may be objected, that the fect adverted to is but comparatively fmall to the reft of chriftendom. But I fee no reafon if this fect in different parts of the world can maintain good order and affectually promote religion without priefts, why all the reft of chriftendom might not do the fame; for the whole body of chriftians is made up of fmaller communities, each of which might do the like. But to thofe who improperly would make numbers an obftacle, it may be recommeded that they take a view of the mahometans, among whom there are no priefts; yet no men entertain a more fervent zeal for their religion (true or falfe is not here the queftion); nor do any perfevere with more vigour in prayer, in fafting, and a long train of incumbrances and feverities attending it, without having fo much as a fingle prieft to exhort or incite them. If therefore fo much is performed without priefts in a religion admitted by all chriftians to be falfe, what might not be effected in like manner by chriftians in a religion that

S   is is true? But such active vigour can never be the produce of establishments, for in establishments the priest has an appointment for a certain duty, which he claims whether he performs that duty or not; the duty therefore is generally much neglected; and the common people especially being taught in the business of religion to rely solely on the priest, they become habitually satisfied with his neglect, which concludes in a torpor of supineness and indifference. Hence in all establishments there is little of the essence of religion, but instead of it occasional form, ceremony, show and parade, sufficient to announce that it is not wholly dead though it be enervated and motionless.—This is no favourable picture of establishments, but I fear it is a true one. If true, there certainly can be no necessity for such establishments, and especially as I think it has been made appear that religion may flourish without priests, at least as well as with them.—The consideration I grant is important and deserves attention; but on a strict and candid enquiry I trust it will be discovered that interest, rather than religion, is the basis of all religious state establishments.— It is a tender case, and too delicate perhaps to be proposed to those who enjoy such emoluments; besides, the time is improper while in

health

health they embrace them: but I could wish to have the sentiments, after due reflection, of a sensible person on this subject immediately on his departure from this world to another, when probably gibes and prevarication would yield to sincerity and truth, on finding he could no longer shun the place

> " Where friends and foe
> " Lie close; unmindful of their former feuds.
> " The lawn-rob'd prelate, and plain presbyter
> " E'er while that stood aloof, as shy to meet,
> " Familiar mingle here, like sister-streams
> " That some rude interposing rock had split."
>
> The Grave, by Blair.

But waving a subject so truly serious, can any man in his senses imagine that the French legislators are not as competent as Mr. B. who officiously intrudes himself, to determine the number of priests necessary for the purposes of religion in their own country, and what ought to be their stipend or appointment? That person surely is an object of pity who being possessed by the spirit of interference engages himself in the concerns of others without an adequate knowledge to sanction the intrusion. It may be alleged that humanity calls forth Mr. B. to plead the cause of so many distressed objects on being discharged from their appointments and functions. It is with reluctance I would call any man's humanity into question; but if an impartial reader will go over his letter he must meet with so many striking passages* of a spirit diametrically opposite to humanity, to good nature, to delicacy, to decency in the treatment of particular persons, and such a licence given to invective both in sentiment and expression, as cannot fail to shock their feelings, while virulence plucks up humanity by the roots to burn it on the altar of malignity. But let us pass over the misnomer, and say these outrages were the effusions of humanity. What then? Does not every one know that in all great revolutions there must be sufferers? were none to suffer, there would have been no need of a revolution, all things being as they should be, right; whereas the intention of a revolution is to reform what is wrong: and it is impossible that in such violent and extensive agitations but that some must receive even an unmerited shock. In cases less formidable than revolutions, the like occurs for the benefit of the state; I can remember when in our own country, in a time too of profound peace and tranquility,

* P. 11, 55, 56, 57, 58, 61, 62, 63, 67, 77, 78, 99, 100, 101, 102, 106, 108, 114, 115, 135, and a variety of other passages, as 158, 159, &c.

quility, many hundred of very reputable citizens were by a single act of parliament thrown out of that business in which they had expended much time and money for instruction, and were in an instant almost turned adrift to seek a livelihood as they could, while neither the legislature nor the rest of mankind conceived that this was in any wise amiss, or thought of making them any compensation.* The French church was surcharged with an unnecessary number of clergy of all denominations; and in the distress of the state, (or even were there no such distress) there could be no reason why opulent indolence should consume in luxury the children's inheritance. The useless hands were therefore dismissed, and as many as were judged useful and necessary, retained, and on competent salaries, by which the interests of religion would be much better promoted than by supplying them with the means of luxury to be employed to the neglect of their function, and the setting the rest of mankind a bad and dangerous precedent by their example. But this prudence, I should rather say sagacity, is travestied by

---

* Alluding to the act which caused the distillers, or rectifiers of malt spirits, almost all of them to a very small number to relinquish their business and shut up their offices throughout the kingdom.

by our author, and converted into a reprefentation exhibiting cruelty and injuftice,* while to ftimulate our fenfibility we are, as I fhould think, ludicroufly informed, that the church made to the ftate a voluntary offer of a large contribution.† That is, thefe holy men made an offer of *part* of thofe riches of which it forefaw it would be difpoffeffed. But if the church on conftraint was fo wonderfully generous *now*, why was it not fomewhat *voluntarily* generous *before*, and why did it not come forth like wife men to make their offerings? This clumfy artifice was therefore juftly treated with con- contempt as a fabrication from the vile manufactories of avarice and deception. They would not relinquifh any part of their luxuries but on compulfion though the ftate ftarved; the ftate they confidered as nothing to them, but fo far as they were gainers by making a property of it; and as to the duties of their office, the principle of which I underftand to be preaching and praying, thofe of the higher orders among them had almoft wholly declined, while many of them were neither from their learning nor mode of living adapted to fuch ftations, but were ftuck there like oftentatious efcutcheons

againft

* P. 156—158. † P. 179.

against a church wall, not with any view to religion, but to indicate they belonged to some great families who through interest had procured them these lucrative and lazy appointments. To dismiss such men was surely not an act of cruelty, but of justice to religion and to the state; and instead of complaining, they might be thankful that they were not sooner discharged not only as unprofitable, but as bad servants, who could give no account of their stewardships but such as directly tended to their condemnation, and the forfeiture of a property so constantly abused that its confiscation was become a measure absolutely requisite for the putting their order under better regulations both with regard to religion and the state. This is the light in which this confiscation of church property appears to me; it meets with my hearty and sincere approbation, and I presume it will be applauded by every candid and impartial friend of mankind who has not resigned up his reason to be led away by sophistry and to be bewildered in chimerical rhapsodies, teeming with bigotted notions of the consacration of kingdoms,* and the sacredness of church-land, and church-men,† to which with equal propriety

---

* P. 136—137. † P. 157.

priety might have been added their induſtrious indolence, the ſanctity of their debaucheries, and the holineſs of their vices.

But though in conſequence of this confiſcation of church property, opulent indolence and pampered oſcitancy and ignorance have been ſent empty away, and a maſs of wealth which was conſtantly imployed in imparting ſtrength to the power of a foreign ſovereign in the kingdom, is now directed to better purpoſes in the ſtate, towards relieving its exigencies; yet as all who have been diſmiſſed come not under that deſcription, I could have wiſhed ſome regard had been paid to ſuch of them as had merit, by a proviſion allotted them according to their rank. But on reflexion, I find this was impracticable. Such a marked and partial diſtinction would have been a freſh ſource of exaſperation. Moſt men conceive as highly at leaſt of themſelves as they do of others; therefore every man would have thought himſelf equally intitled, and on being refuſed might ſay, Is it not enough that you injure me, without adding inſult to injury? It would alſo have been highly impolitic, for each perſon who was diſmiſſed would not only conceive himſelf injured as an individual, but he would feel and reſent

resent it for the whole body, and no charm of private gratuity would be able to stifle such resentment; to have given such gratuity therefore would have been like putting arms into their hands, which they would have employed in resisting their adversaries; and not to grant it, was of course providing for their own security. The National Assembly could not be unacquainted with the general character of this body of men; that it possesses a characteristic is not singular, whatever the particular character may be; most communities are so, from the largest to the smallest. Thus nations are characteristic, we speak without reserve of the *hauteur* of the Spaniard; punick faith was proverbial; in Virgil * we read, *Timeo Danaos et dona ferentes;* the Cretans are marked by Paul† as very deficient in point of veracity; and lastly, not to enter into useless enumerations, the name John Bull, which has been applied to us, or which we have applied to ourselves, characterizes the sturdy bluntness of our own countrymen. As nations are characteristic, so are smaller societies, and it would be not only unnecessary but invidious to explain what must occur to every one, especially in treating of smaller communities. Of

T that

---

* Æn. ii. v. 49. † To Titus, ch. i. v. 12.

that community however which is under confideration fomething muft be faid. Davila, the hiftorian of the civil wars of France, and who cannot be fuppofed to caft unmerited reproach on the priefts of his own perfuafion, reprefents them as audacioufly violent in fupport of their own caufe or intereft; no extremities confined them, nor would they be deterred by force or reafon from obtaining their ends while the profpect afforded a glimpfe of fuccefs. Their activity induced them to publifh falfities from their pulpits to inflame the people.* They fcandalized in their preachments without refpect to character or rank.† They filled the ears of the populace with inflammatory tales to fan the flames of civil difcord.‡ And again, they thunder

---

* *Le quali cofe intonando da' pulpiti i loro predicatori, empiveno il popolo di vano terrore, e d' acerbiffimo odio contra alla perfone del principe, e contra a' configlieri, e favoriti fuoi.*
Davila, delle Guerre Civ. di Francia. Lib. vii. p. 446.

† *Entrava egli molte volte in penfiero di caftigare la temerità di coftoro, e di vendicarfi così dello fprezzo, che moftravano i predicatori, fparlando in publico della perfona fua, come delle congiurati di quefti follevatori del popolo, che li havevano rivoltata contra la maggior, e più confidente citta del regno fuo, mà mille cofe lo ritenevano.* Id. ib. lib. viii. p. 518.

‡ *Ed i predicatori con le maniere folite, mà con maggior licenza fparlando apertamente delle cofe prefenti, empivano. L'orecchie del*

der from their pulpits the eulogies of their favourites for the fame purpofe; exciting the populace to ferocity and revenge.* Their preachments probably, but certainly the advife of fome of their orders, inftigate, not merely to common murther, but even to regicide;† and the attempt

---

popolo delle maraviglie, anzi de' miracoli, cosè li chiamavano, di quefto nuovo Gedeone, venuto al mondo per la defiderata falvezza della Francia. Id. ib. lib. ix. p. 570.

* *Intonarono i predicatori da' pulpiti la medefima fera, ed il giorno feguente, le lodi del marterio del Duca di Guifa, e le deteftationi della ftrage commeffa crudelmente dal Rì, di modo, che gli animi non folo della infima plebe, mà anco de' più confpicui trà i cittadini reftarono ingombrati dalle loro ragioni ed accefi di grandiffimo defiderio di farne la vendetta; il quale ardire, e ne' predicatori, e nel popolo fi raddoppiò quando fopragiunfe la nuova della morte del Cardinale, la quale finè di ridurre gli animi all' ultima efferazione.* Id. ib. lib. x. p. 4.——*Havere con patienza inaudita tollerate l' ingiurie de' popoli, le invettive de' predicatori, le villane infolenze de' fattiofi, i decreti temerarii della Sorbona.* Id. ib. lib. x. p. 23. *I predecatori, benchè molto caduti di animo, e di riputatione, attendevano ad inanimire il popolo, il quale manifeftamente fi vedeva meflo, ed avvilito.* Id. ib. lib. x. p. 49.

† *Giacopo Clemente dell' ordine di San Domenico—ò guidato dalla propria fantafia, ò ftimulato dalle predicationi, che giornalmente fentiva fare contra Henrico di Valois nominato il perfecutore della fede, ed il tiranno; prefe rifolutione di voler pericolare la fua vita per tentare in alcuna maniera d'ammazzarlo, nè tenne fegreto quefto così temerario penfiero, ma andava vociferando trà fuoi, che*

tempt was made with all coolness and deliberation, by plunging a knife into the king's body,* of which wound he died soon after; yet the preachers applauded the assassination, and commended in high terms, from their pulpits. the assassin.

era necessario d'adoperare l'armi, e di esterminare il tiranno—disse ad un padre de' suoi, che haveva una inspiratione gagliarda di andare ad amazzare Henrico di Valois, e che dovesse consigliarlo, se la dovesse eseguire. Il padre conferito il fatto con il priore, il quale era uno de' principali consiglieri della lega, risposero unitamente, che vedesse bene, che questa non fosse una tentatione del demonio, che digiunasse ed orasse, pregando il Signore che gl' illuminasse la mente di quello doveva operare. Tornò frà pochi giorni costui al priore, ed al altro padre, dicendo loro, che haveva fatto quanto gli havevano consigliato, e che sentiva più spirito che mai di volere intraprendere questo fatto. I Padri, come molti dissero, conferito il negotio con Madama di Mompensieri, ò come vogliono quei della lega, di proprio loro motivo l'esortarono al tentativo, affermandoli, che vivendo sarebbe stato fatto Cardinale, e morendo per haver liberata la città, ed ucciso il persecutore della fede, sarebbe senza dubbio canonizato per Santo. Id. ib. lib. x. p. 50, 51.

* *Introdotto il Frate, mentre si ritirava quasi due a canto ad una finestra, porse la lettera del conte di Brienna, la quale letta haven dogli detto il Rè, che sognasse a spiegargli il suo negotio, egli finse di metter mano ad un'altra carta per presentarla, e mentre il Rè intentamente l'aspetta, cavatosi il solito coltello dalla manica, lo ferè a canto, all' umbelico della parte sinistra, e lasciò tutto il ferro confitto nella ferita.* Id. ib. lib. x. p. 52.

affaffin.* Fired with fuch zeal in fupport of their interefts, we are not to be furprized that they excited the people to take arms, nor even that they themfelves bore them.† Nor yet that they fhould grant abfolution for known deliberate murther,‡ which however his holinefs would

* Trà i quali il Padre Edmondo Borgoino priore di Frati di San Domenico, il quale convinto da teftimonii d'haver lodato publicamente in pergamo l'homicidio commeffo nelle perfona de Rè, e d'haver configliato, ed inftigato il percuffore, comparandolo anco dopo il fatto nelle fue prediche a Giudit, il Rè morto ad Oloferne, la citta liberata a Betulia, fù per fentenza de parlamento di Turs fententiato a effere da quattro cavalli fbranato, le membre abbruciate, e fparfe le ceneri al vento. Id. ib. lib. x. p. 68.—E. Padre Roberto Francifcano, che haveva quivi publicamente lodato la morte del Rè, e felevvata con le fue predicationi la plebe, furono condannati allo morte. Id. ib. lib. x. p. 90.

† Monfignore di Reno facendo ufficio di maftro di campo generale fcorreva per ogni luogo, e i preti, e i frati concorrendo alle fattioni militari popolarmente, havevano prefe l'armi. Id. ib. lib. x. p. 49.—Edivifo in più bande, fecondo la divifione dei quartieri, s'apprefentava volonterofo e pronto a tu te le fattioni, e con l'efempio de' Preti, e de' Frati, i quali armati falivano le muraglie, e s'adoperavano in tutte le cofe con ammirabile coftanza. Id. ib. lib. xi. p. 147.

‡ Per la qual cofa, fe bene in virtù di un Breve conceffoli dal papa prefente pochi mefi prima, di poterfi far affolvere di ogni cofo rifervato dal fuo fuo confeffore, fi haveva fatto dare l'affolutione della morte del cardinale, nondimeno vedendo che quefto non baftava, fpedì Claudio d'Angene della famiglia fua favorita di Rhamburghefio Vefcovo di Mans, huomo di profonda literatura, e di fingular eloquenza, acciochè informato di tutte le ragioni, come fuo procuratore ricevegge l'affoluti... de l Pontefice. Id. ib. lib. x. p. 17.

would not confirm but on political confiderations and advantages.* The zeal of the prelates was alfo of a fimilar complexion; againſt the remonſtrances, not even the threatenings of his holinefs, nor the caufe of religion had any weight, when they found it was more conducive to their intereſt to join the party of the king; at the fame time intimating that there were feafons when the earneſt wiſhes of his holinefs might be complied with, but that it was unreafonable to expect it now that his majefty's affairs

* Non havendo mai havuta intentione d'offendere la giurifdittione della feda Apoſtolica, dopo che gli n' era ſtata fatta cofcienza, moſſo da interno fcrupolo, s'era proſtrato a' piedi del confeſſore, e havea chieſta e impetrata l'affolutione, perquanto faceſſe bifogno, benchè ſtimoſſe de non haver effettuamente trafgredito. A queſto rifpofe il pontefice, che il breve era conceſſo per le cofe paſſate, ma che non fi poteva eſtendere a' peccati futuri de' quali non ſi può anticipare l'affolutione—Effendo ſi molte volte repetita, e con grande allegation d'autorità e di ragioni, diſcuſſa queſta trattatione, finalmente gli ambaſceatori condeſcefere a contentarſe a dimandar in ifcritto l'affolutione del papa, il quale moſtrava defiderarla, per mezzo di effa dover reſtar placato e fodisfatto; per la qual cofa dopo gli uficii paſſati da gli ambaſciatori di Venezia e di Toſcana a favore del Rè, che ſe ne affaticarono fommamente per ordine de' loro principi il vefcovo con fupplica eſtefa in forma di multa fommiſſione dimandò al pontefice l'affolutione, il quale con parole piacevoli rifpofe, che volentieri l'harebbe conceſſa, quando foſſe ſtato ſicuro della contritione del Rè, della quale voleva queſto fegno, che poneſſe in libertà il cardinale di Borbone, e l'Archiveſcovo di Lione.

Id. ib. l.b. x. p. 18, 19.

affairs were in fo profperous a fituation.*—In what has been here advanced the reader will be pleafed to take notice that it is not I who fpeak, the authorities are given, and the words of the author; in doing which a few paffages only are felected from a great variety of the fame tendency: but thefe are fufficient to give fome idea of the defcription of thofe perfons in the general, with which the National Affembly had to deal when it confifcated church property. It is in vain to tell us that I have been fpeaking of perfons who lived two centuries ago. I anfwer, that I have been treating of communities which exifted

---

* *Confideravano i Signori Francefi effer cofa non folo difficile, mà da non fperarla per alcun modo, che i prelati e la nobiltà, i quali bavevano nelle mani del Rè la roba, le dignità, e le prelature rifolveffero d'abbandonarle per compiacere il papa, effendo pochi a i tempi prefenti coloro che per rifpetto dell'anima fi contentino di abandonare le loro foftanze; ch'effi già da principio s'erano d'avvantaggio reffigurate quefte minaccie, e quefte intimazioni di Roma, s'havevano preparato gli animi per foffrirle; che fra che fi sforzaffero, più s'indurerebbono, e perdendo la fperanza d'effere ricevuti mai in gratie del papa, fi farebbero più oftinati a fignalare, ed a procurare la vittoria alla loro parte; che bifognava allettarli, e deftramenti tirarli, non fpaventarli, e metterli nell'ultima difperazione; che fimil minacchie farebbono proprie di chi la vittoria per dare loro colore ed occafione di abandonare con quefto pretefto il Rè, quando le cofe fue foffero deplorate, ù non bora, ch'effendo egli fiorido e potente, non era da credere, s'alcuno le abbandonaffe.* Id. ib. lib. xii p. 221.

existed from that time, till this event; that communities rarely, if ever, lose their original character, that they had maintained the same character for many centuries before, and that two centuries is a very short period with respect to communities for divesting themselves of their original character. I am ready to admit they may undergo some variation in the *degree*, but still the same character remains though in a different degree; but that degree cannot be ascertained till opportunity presents them the power of acting. As the National Assembly had determined to establish the revolution, it could not leave the church property in these hands, nor could it safely pension such of them as had merit, nor could it do otherwise than dissolve these societies. While connected, they were a formidable body acting by one will; and as their function established an intercourse with all ranks and degrees, they might be highly dangerous to the revolution; to have left in their hands property of any kind, which is only another name for power, would have increased the danger; so that confiscation and dismission, if the revolution was to stand on a firm basis, became absolutely necessary and unavoidable: and I persuade myself the revolution would have had much more to apprehend from these men if

continued

continued in their former ſtate, than from all their other adverſaries combined together. But I ſhall add nothing more, than that if the revolution was to ſtand, theſe men muſt fall.

As Mr. B. has opened to us a ſpacious field, and well ſtocked, I ſhall now decline this purſuit for ſome other game, and endeavour in the poet's phraſe to " ſhoot folly as it flies ;" " we " look up," ſays he, " with awe to kings:"* Some perſons may think it a misfortune, this doctrine was not promulgated before Beckford went up with his petition; for awe was ſo far from his thoughts, that after delivering it he ſtood reaſoning and remonſtrating; as the ſcroll to his ſtatue teſtifies to this day; and as that ſtatue was erected at the expence of the city of London, it evinces that this doctrine of awe was not known and practiſed there at that time.——— Let us take a candid view of the hiſtory of kings, and ſee if their general character does not excite in us ſomething of a very different complexion from awe. Is Mr. B.'s memory treacherous, or does he mean to mock mankind; his own doctrine on this ſubject formally delivered, puts every thing in the ſhape or ſem-

* P. 129.

blance of awe wholly out of the queſtion; we cannot entertain awe for thoſe who have ſo little regard to their own character as to delight in " mean company;" we may behold ſuch objects with pity, but he who entertains pity is ſuperior to awe.—It was obſerved at page 74 of this work, that Mr. B. had improved upon ancient ethics and had favoured the world with a new doctrine; he here comes forward as an additional apoſtle, or one improving on the old ſtandard; for the words of the apoſtle are in all my editions " Fear God, honour the king;"* but Mr. B.'s doctrine is, " Fear God, ſtand in " awe of kings:" awe or dread implies fear in the exceſs, ſo that by this doctine of Mr. B. our ſubmiſſion to kings is greater than that which is due to God himſelf. No one the leaſt acquainted with the Engliſh language will aſſent, that fear and awe are convertible terms; but were they ſo, even then our author places God and kings on the ſame parallel. Without affecting a nicer conſcience or more religion than every perſon ought to poſſeſs, Mr. B. will excuſe me if I cannot pledge him in this " cup of " abomination"† and idolatry. With the character of a courtier, agreeably to Monteſquieu's deſcription,

---

* 1 Peter, ch. ii. v. 17.　　† P. 156.

description, it may be compatible; or it may be consistent with the ideas of those who " desire " honours, distinctions, and emoluments, but " little,"* to hold forth this draught to mankind and ingratiate themselves with those who have these trumperies at their disposal; but such as have a sense of their duty to heaven, and who claim little more than *mens sana in corpore sano*, and which kings have not to bestow, will dash this irreligious cup to the ground with horror, leaving the impious dregs to be licked up with the dust by reprobates.

Knowledge, even that small portion of it that can be acquired, is the fruit of much labour, observation, time and experience; the station, modern education, and mode of life of princes, rarely supplies them with any tolerable share of it. Hence flatterers, their greatest enemies, make them an easy prey; and the softer the matter they have to work upon, the deeper is the impression. If there is no political vice in the character of a prince, great allowance ought to be made for deficiencies, which are rather a failure than a fault. But not one grain of lenity is due to their flatterers who taking advantage

---

* Pult.

of their foibles, and with a view to private emolument, would endeavour to perfuade them they are, what they are not. A good king, and a wife one, are two diftinct beings; I prefer a good, to a wife king; becaufe goodnefs of heart is likely to be more beneficial to the people than the goodnefs of the head, which often leads both themfelves and others into perilous difficulties,* while from the former their flows a conftant and full ftream of tranquility and beneficence. The perfect character is to be wife and good, but this is a character we have no right to expect; and when it does come, it fhould be confidered as a prodigy: if he be but good I honour him; my duty demands it; and it would be unjuft and ungenerous, not to fay folly and weaknefs, confidering the mamy difadvantages under which he labours; or rather the many opportunities of which he is deprived, to expect to fee a king wifer than the reft of mankind. The treafure of wifdom was never intended to be the poffeffion of

all

---

* Charles the Firft had the *reputation* of being a wife prince, but his wifdom tended to nothing fo effectually as to embroil him with his fubjects, and to be productive of a fatal end to himfelf; and he died a *martyr* to his wifdom or obftinancy.— I could point to one or two more *reputed* wife fovereigns in Europe, whofe wifdom centered in lavifhing the blood and treafure of their fubjects. But the criterion of a good prince are peace, harmony, beneficence.

all men; but it is expected of all men that they should be good, and all men have wisdom enough, though not the will, to be good.—Therefore I honour a king if he be but good, but I do not look up with awe to any king but the King of Heaven. From a bad king I avert my fight, as from a thing that is odious and insufferable; because he has it in his power to be good; his station in a particular manner requires it of him; and his not being so, will most probably be productive of the greatest mischief. This lesson, perhaps, will be acceptable to few of them; but I trust it is more ingenuous than any they are likely to meet with in the whole range of their courtiers; and happy may such be who attend to it.

Before we relinquish this subject it is necessary to advert to a passage in Mr. B.'s letter, which as it seems to contain some latent meaning, it may be proper to call it forth to public view and examine it. He says " Our constitution " has made no sort of provision towards render- " ing him (the king) as a servant, in any de- " gree responsible." * Does Mr. B. here mean to say that our kings are not responsible; or, does he employ the words " as a servant " for a disguise

* P. 42.

disguise or subterfuge, thereby meaning, that he is not responsible *as a servant,** but yet he is responsible. If the latter be his meaning, it is nothing better than a petty quibbling about terms, and by which the fact is no wise affected. Now he either is responsible, or he is not so. If he is responsible, he is so to some person, or some body of men, for it would be ridiculous to affirm that a person is responsible, and yet that there are none to whom he is so; and if he be but responsible, it is wholly immaterial under what character or appellation, whether as a servant, agent, or under any other name. The question therefore is, Is he responsible? and this Mr. B. though he starts the subject, endeavours to evade by misleading us, affirming that he is not responsible *as a servant,* which determines nothing concerning his responsibility in any other character;

---

* The author of *Anti-Machiavel*, whom no one doubts was the late King of Prussia, in speaking on this subject, says, *Le Souverain, bien loin d'être le maître absolu des peuples qui sont sous sa domination, n'en est que le prémier Magistrat.* Anti-Mach. ch. i. p. 2. " The Sovereign, very far from being the abso-" lute master of the people under his government, is but their " chief magistrate." And I must confess I understand all magistrates, though in different degrees, to be the servants of the public. But all this is no more than cavilling about terms: for the fact is, that each is responsible, under whatever denomination he holds a trust.

character; and we want to know whether he is at all refponfible, becaufe that infinuation feems to be held forth rather as implying that he is not. Now to clear up this matter, if it be afferted that he is not refponfible, I would wifh to know how James the IId came to flee this kingdom; was not his reafon for fo doing, becaufe he was convinced that he was refponfible, and he would not wait the event of becoming accountable for his actions. Again, if kings are not refponfible, with what propriety can Mr. B. fay, " The pu-" nifhment of tyrants is a noble and aweful act " of juftice."* But how fo, and where is the juftice? for though a tyrant, he is ftill a king; none I prefume will deny that Henry the VIIIth was a tyrant, nor will they deny he was a king; as being a tyrant therefore does not deftroy the title and character of king, and kings are not refponfible, where is the juftice of this punifhment. It is not meant furely to punifh without calling to account. If you mean to call them to account, you have no right to do fo; how can you call to account him who is not refponfible; and if you call him to account, and punifh, it is an act of injuftice, becaufe he is not refponfible. And laftly, to fay that a king

is

* P. 123 and 157.

is not refponfible, is only in other terms to affert that he is defpotic. If a king is not refponfible, he may certainly act and do whatever he pleafes; and in the three following defcriptions of men I would gladly be informed where is the difference between a prince who acts and does whatever he pleafes, a prince who is not refponfible, and a defpotic prince; the only difference is in the letters and found of the terms, while in fact each and all of them imply one and the fame thing: for he that is not refponfible, may act and do what he pleafes, with impunity; can any defpotic prince do more? As this fubject ftarted by Mr. B. appears to be clogged with a hefitation, or rather a falfe bias has been given to it, I judged it advifable to guard all parties from error by giving it a difcuffion, the refult of which is, that every prince who is not refponfible is defpotic; and as there is no defpotic power in this country, the prince therefore is refponfible.——There is another maxim nearly allied to this fubject, I fpeak not of it as coming from Mr. B. but as the affinity is fo great, it fhould not be paffed over in filence; it is included in thefe fix important words, The king can do no wrong. This maxim appears to me to have been fabricated by perfidious or flattering ftatefmen. I would it were as true, as it

is

is falfe. A king may do much wrong, much evil; I have it not in my nature to deny what fact and experience daily evince; and this he may do with or without the advice of counfellors; and to fay that, for what is fo done by their advice, they alone are refponfible, is as unjuft and partial a determination as the maxim itfelf is falfe, becaufe it tends at moft to the punifhing of a part only inftead of the whole; but generally ends in the punifhment of none, as they elude their deferts by their power and influence, and that of thofe connected with them in the mifchief.———By a fimilar defcription of men, for they abound in all courts, and in times of ignorance, which is their only excufe, they wrefted from the King of Heaven his attributes and titles, difpofed of them to a mere mortal, and hailed him " Sovereign Lord the King;" * as though by this profane fporting with titles, he had in the inftant changed his nature, and put on immortality. To thefe *human* divinities the deluded populace led on by artful parafites, and bigotted priefts, might " look up with awe," and entertain a veneration for them, fimilar to that which the vulgar among the heathens expreffed for their deities, though contaminated

with

* P. 141.

with all the vices that can blot, deface, and degrade human nature. But it is to be presumed that since those days of ignorance the prince, the priest, and the people, have undergone a compleat transmutation by the alchemy of the times: if not, I trust that old alchemist will not desist from his labours till the transmutation is perfect.

Mr. B. complains of falacies concealed under terms employed by others, " It would require," says he, " a long discourse to point out to you the " many fallacies that lurk in the generality and " equivocal nature of the terms *inadequate re-* " *presentation*."* But of all didactic writers I ever read, no one to the best of my recollection ever used terms in so vague and indeterminate a manner as Mr. B. I do not remember that he employs one definition, though he uses terms in a manner very different from the rest of mankind, and in a mode which appears to me exceptionable. I am led to this observation by the following passage, " I shall only say here " in justice to that old fashioned constitution, " under which we have long prospered."† I would willingly understand what it is he meant
should

* P. 83.   † P. 83.

should be underſtood by the terms " old-" faſhioned conſtitution," and, " we have long " proſpered;" if he means, that ſyſtem of laws and original mode of government uſed in this kingdom, I ſhould anſwer, they are no more, but in a manner totally done away, and are ſo continually changing and fluctuating that the traces of what he adverts to are hardly to be found. Let us take a tranſcient view of our proſperity under what he calls the old-faſhioned government or conſtitution, by which we have been ſo long proſperous down to the preſent hour. Not to go too far back, we may firſt obſerve the people were reduced to the dreadful neceſſity of diſpatching one king, and of expelling another; in the reign of George the firſt there was a deeply concerted rebellion to deprive him of the throne; and in the ſucceeding reign there was another, when the rebels entered England and put the whole kingdom into a conſternation.—Either that old-faſhioned conſtitution is not retained, or we are not altogether ſo proſperous under it, or both; while for annual parliaments, we have now ſeptennial ones; for a few laws which inflicted capital puniſhment, the number is now almoſt innumerable; the exciſe laws which are daily increaſing have trampled down and almoſt exterminated

terminated both the ancient law and liberty of the subject, and a thousand other violences have been committed against the old constitution, so that the constitution we now have is either a new one, or the old one so totally defaced and mutilated as to be with difficulty recognized in our present situation; and yet Mr. B. as in derision, is applauding our prosperous state under the old constitution, as though we still possessed it. The old constitution I make no doubt might have been improved as all which is the product of humanity may be meliorated, human nature producing nothing that is perfect; but the old constitution has been totally vitiated, and our *prosperous* state is the consequence. Our present prosperous situation resembles that of a heedless country squire who has mortgaged the whole of his patrimony for nearly the value. The importunate tax-gatherer is never out of our houses, collecting money for the light of heaven, and diving into our pockets for the last solitary shilling, while water and air remain the almost only articles untaxed in the kingdom. We have a stupendous debt which can only be enumerated by hundreds of millions of pounds sterling; the sum is so vast, that a tolerable arithmetician can hardly obtain a clear and distinct idea of it; and the weight is

so

so oppreffive to the nation, that it rocks from one fide to the other threatening " hideous " ruin," not lefs agitated than Ætna when tortured by her convulfive fires: but we are not left comfortefs, this national debt is paying off under this old conftitution with a profpect as promifing as that of employing an ant to carry away by atoms the rock of Gibraltar. We are fo very profperous that Spain alone and on her fole ftrength dares menace us without our giving the leaft provocation, put us to the charge of fitting out a great armament, and then in derifion as our ftate is fo profperous leave us to bear all the expence of it. Part too of our profperity according to this capricious and paradoxical writer muft confift in our lofs of America, which to fay nothing farther fupplied us with excellent failors and foldiers, who to us are now no more, unlefs as adverfaries. The flowing tide of this our profperity has for fome time paft run fo high that fhould it continue for the next half century, having no longer fufficient mounds to oppofe it, we muft be deluged. In fhort, I tremble for the guzzling down of this profperity in fuch large and frequent draughts; I fear it muft in the end intoxicate, and there is no anfwering for what men fo intoxicated may not do.—Thefe are

some

some of the blessings derived to us under this old or new-fashioned constitution, for call it by what name you please, neither the fashion nor the effects of it are thereby altered or abated; and whoever stiles this a state of prosperity has very different ideas of a state of prosperity from those which I entertain, and I should presume too from those of the rest of mankind. It presents us with a picture representing to our view a dissipating heir consuming with jollity and glee the last lonely guinea of the squandered inheritance, in defiance of that distress which must be the certain and inevitable consequence; while an arch rogue who longs to partake of it, applauds the measure, and reminds him how long he has prospered by pursuing this practice.—As to the constitution I here determine nothing concerning it; what I assert is this, If it be good, a very bad use must have been made of it to reduce us to the unprosperous state in which we now are; and then, *Rebus autem afflictis cum patriam obsederi audissit, non quisivit ubi tuto viveret*, that is he sought not "honours, distinc-" tions, and emoluments," to the gratification of his avarice or ambition, *sed unde praesidio posset esse civibus suis.** And if it be bad, then

Consulite

* Nep. in vita Canonis.

*Confulite in medium, et rebus fuccurrite veſtris.**

There certainly is fomething wrong fomewhere, egregiouſly wrong, as will be feen on the application of this concife ſtatement in the words of Salluſt: *Profectò virtus atque ſapientia major in illis freit, qui exparvis opibus tantum imperium fecére, quàm in nobis qui ea bene parta vix retinemus.*† To what purpofe then is trumpeted forth to us the encomium on "this old-fafhioned "conſtitution under which we have long profpered," unlefs it be to infult the fenfes and underſtandings of mankind!

Mr. B. with an air of fuperiority and contempt, afks "who now reads Bolingbroke? "who ever read him through?"‡ And again, "I do not often quote Bolingbroke, nor have "his works in general made any permanent "impreffion on my mind. He is a prefumptuous and fuperficial writer."§ I could wifh this prefumption and fuperficiality had refted there; but I find that men in point of literature, are like women in refpect to beauty, blind to their own imperfections. I will frankly acknowledge I have read Bolingbroke through and

---

* Virg. Æn. xi. v. 335.   † Sal. Bell. Cat.   ‡ P. 133.
§ P. 187.

and have been highly gratified. Some of his works I have read more than once: and part of the knowledge he has communicated has made a deep and permanent impreſſion on my mind. Amidſt a great variety of inſtructive, and entertaining matter in many of his works, his letter to Sir William Windham appears to me excellent; in that private hiſtory great light is thrown upon ſome important tranſactions of thoſe times, not omitting thoſe which preceded, and in the former of which he was no inconſiderable agent. Among many other intereſting events, it exhibits a uſeful leſſon in his own perſon of a wiſe man completely duped by a ſet of fools and knaves. The characters of Charles and James are finely contraſted, and though given by a few ſtrokes are a maſter-piece in that kind of painting. I cannot refrain laying them before my reader with the introduction. "The exile," ſays he, "of the royal family, under Cromwell's uſurpa-
"tion, was the principal cauſe of all thoſe miſ-
"fortunes in which Britain has been involved,
"as well as of many of thoſe which have hap-
"pened to the reſt of Europe, during more
"than half a century."

"The two brothers, Charles and James, be-
"came then infected with popery to ſuch degrees,

" grees, as their different characters admitted
" of. Charles had parts; and his good under-
" standing served as an antidote to repel the
" poison. James, the simplest man of his time,
" drank off the whole chalice. The poison
" met, in his composition with all the fear, all
" the credulity, and all the obstinacy of temper
" proper to increase its virulence, and to
" strengthen its effect—."* I do not conceive
that the person who writes in this stile is so de-
spicable a writer; but I am neither Bolingbroke's critic, nor his second; he has his ble-
mishes and his beauties, but he who traduces
him as a writer mistakes his own way to literary
fame. I profess to know but little of men or
books; there appears to me to be no criterion
or standard to regulate and determine such judgment, while we see one praises what another
condemns with equal plausibility. My own in-
ability is countenanced by that of others; and
as Mr. B. speaks freely of Bolingbroke, which
is but matter of opinion, I shall not hesitate to
take into consideration the abilities of the author
of that opinion, that we may know how far it
may be relied on. I have no doubt Mr. B. is
a great reader; he appears to me to have collected

* Bolingbroke, letter to Sir W. Windham, p. 288. 289.

lected and amassed from all quarters good and bad indiscriminately, a large mass of indigested matter, with which his mind is surcharged, and from which it labours at times to be relieved. Acquired without selection, retained without arangement it forms a confused chaos; and instead of invigorating the mind, like an exuberance of flesh in the human body, tends only to render it more unweildy and fuller of humours. Hence that inequality so obvious in all he writes or speaks; hence strange doctrines, and still stranger conclusions; eccentric sentiments delivered in exaggerated, tortured, and distorted language, one while elevated and carried beyond the sublime into the bombast, at other times meanly creeping and licking the dust; metaphors injudiciously chosen, improperly applied, and sometimes disgusting from the unnecessary horror they convey, at other times from the offensive and indelicate ideas they excite; rancor wrapped up in foul language; affected pathos worked into puerility; petty antethesis apologizes for wit; a jingle of words is substituted for sense: all this, and much more, which certainly are not the characteristics of bright talents, are here to be found; they are the natural result of a plodding mind, long engaged in storing heaps of heterogeneous matter which

it

it cannot aſſort, arrange, or ſelect for uſe, as the exigency may require; nor can it be expected that purer or clearer ſtreams ſhould flow, till the rubbiſh which diſturbs and pollutes the fountain-head is removed. Notwithſtanding this, I make no queſtion but Mr. B. conceives his production will acquire him literary fame, and I well know how ſuch fame is frequently acquired; yet I cannot but obſerve, that to harrangue, and to write are two things very diſtinct; all who harrangue are not good writers, nor do all who harrangue much, ſpeak or write well. Bolingbroke, whom he contemns, appears to me upon the whole to poſſeſs great merit, the knowledge he imparts on many ſubjects is highly inſtructive and intereſting; he had an extenſive underſtanding, and good judgment; and I apprehend he not only is read, but will be read and admired too for his ſtrength of thought, glowing imagination, and unaffected, manly, nervous diction, with all its inaccuracies, when the letter on the French Revolution will ſlink off the public ſtage, and take refuge

In vicum vendentem thus et odores,
Et piper, et quicquid chartis amicitur ineptis;
Hor. Ep. i. lib. 2.

even though gorgeouſly bound in red morocco.

This indignant spurning of Bolingbroke in his grave, reminds me of the fable of the afs kicking a dead lion, at whofe voice, fays the writer, when living he would have been panic-ftruck. The adage of Horace is certainly not amifs,

Metiri fe quemque fuo modulo, ac pede, verum eft.

When I began, I propofed only giving fome few animadverfions on this letter; I have been infenfibly induced to make many; I cannot therefore, confiftently with that propofal, proceed farther. I might apprehend too, left in the progrefs I fhould contract from my author a taint for vilifying, which I fufpect is coming upon me, and by longer contact might prove irrefiftible. I fhall therefore, after making one reflection, drop the pen.——If Mr. B. could have any the moft diftant idea that mankind paid ever fo little deference to his opinion delivered in a publication, whatever he might privately communicate to a friend, he could not confiftently with humanity have publifhed this letter. For if only one half of the French nation had his abilities as a ftatefman or politician in any eftimation, the conftant repetition of degrading, vilifying and inflammatory paffages directed againft the principal perfons who fupport the revolution, muft inevitably have been

productive

productive of such discord throughout that nation as would have been followed by the most tragical events. The scenes of confusion and horror might have been unutterable: It is however a consolation to all who rejoice not in those miseries which afflict mankind, in desolation, destruction, and death, to find that the good sense of that nation is not to be perverted by a composition teeming with rhapsody and wild enthusiasm, which has had no other effect on *their* understanding, than it has with the candid and rational among ourselves; and so far from operating with violence to their injury, has not as yet produced a bloody nose or a scratched face, but on the contrary, was received with pity as the effusion of a brain suffering under the distracting impulse of knight-errantry.

F I N I S.

www.ingramcontent.com/pod-product-compliance
Lightning Source LLC
Chambersburg PA
CBHW020300170426
43202CB00008B/444